The Woman You Want To Be

How To Rise From The Ashes Of An Abusive Relationship

Dr Annie Kaszina Ph.D.

Copyright

Copyright © 2018 Annie Kaszina

Lulu Print Edition

All rights reserved.

ISBN: 978-0-244-71826-8

This book is not intended to provide personalized relationship advice. The Author and the Publisher specifically disclaim any liability, loss or risk which is incurred as a consequence, directly or indirectly, of the use and application of any contents of this work.

Published by: Virtual Precision

Printed and bound in Great Britain.

No part of this work may be reproduced in any material form (including photocopying or storing in any medium by electronic means and whether or not transiently or incidentally to some other use of this publication), without the written permission of the copyright holder, except in accordance with the provisions of the copyright, Designs and Patents Act 1988. Applications for the copyright holders' written permission to reproduce any part of this publication should be addressed to the publisher.

Dedication

*To every woman who walks the journey of healing
from an abusive relationship.
You are so much stronger, braver and more beautiful
than you know.*

Contents

Copyright 2

Dedication 3

Contents 4

Foreword 6

   Chapter 1 13

      Only Invest… 13

   Chapter 2 19

      The Path to Self-Recovery 19

   Chapter 3 25

      Only Celebrate… 25

   Chapter 4 53

      Only See… 53

   Chapter 5 81

      You Are Your Voice 81

   Chapter 6 108

      The Message Unheeded 108

Chapter 7 133
    Being the Difference 133
Chapter 8 161
    Embrace the Miraculous.................................. 161
Chapter 9 185
    Expect Abundance 185
Chapter 10 212
    You Are the Armorer....................................... 212
Chapter 11 238
    Only Allow… 238
Chapter 12 266
    I Am a Miracle... 266
Next Steps... 269

Foreword

As you embark on this journey of healing and self-discovery, you may have things on your mind – like whether you can really move beyond what you have been through to peace of mind, self-worth and a rewarding existence.

You may also be wondering how I am qualified to be your guide. You may just want to be *"introduced"* before we start spending time together.

So, it seems only right to share a little about myself, with a view to getting those considerations out of the way before we really get started. Even though it means talking a bit about me *(even though "me" is not my favorite subject)*, when this book is actually all about you.

If you just want to get started and will decide later whether or not you want to hear about me, then please skip this foreword and dive straight in. If, on the other hand, you have a wee bit of self-talk going on about what is and is not possible for you, I invite you to stick around. This won't take long.

I'm Annie Kaszina. I'm a women's emotional abuse recovery coach, and I am delighted to have this opportunity to work with you. I've been doing this work for 15 years now, helping women all over the world. I chose this field of work because I could not bear to think of all the women who had been deeply wounded by abusive and narcissistic partners and were walking around the world, not getting the help they need.

I know just how difficult it is to be one of those women because I was one.

After 20+ years in an emotionally abusive relationship, I finally got out. Life was better outside the marriage, no doubt about that. However, most of the time, I still felt terrible about myself. I wasn't happy. I lived in a state of constant anxiety. My self-esteem was non-existent. I did not know who I was. I felt like my life was over. Life was tough.

What made it even tougher were the people telling me how I should feel and what I should be doing. If I hadn't felt so terrible about myself, I doubtless would have felt - and done - exactly what they said. But when you are walking around most of the time under a very dark cloud, it is hard to be positive, proactive and resilient. (Some days, it is hard just to drag yourself out of bed in the morning. And nobody gives you credit for what you have achieved when you do.)

That's where this book, *"The Woman You Want To Be"* came from. Obviously, since I don't know you, personally, I can't know exactly what your experiences were. But here's what I do know…

Women who have been through the kind of damaging experiences that you have been through need time, space and kindness to heal.

The question at the forefront of my mind in writing this was,

"What can you – realistically - do to lift and motivate yourself, when you feel hopeless, broken, worthless and at rock bottom?"

Healing is never linear. Nor does it happen overnight. That can be discouraging – especially if you are not expecting the wobbles, the groundhog moments and the relapses. That is why time, space and kindness are so important.

There is another important aspect, also. Anyone who has ended up staying with a horrible partner for any length of time does so, in part, because they have a bit of an Invisibility Habit. (I could have won prizes for Invisibility – if only the real world awarded prizes for invisibility. But, as both know, it does not.)

The time has come for your Invisibility Habit to go. In the past, it may have served you. But not any more.

An essential part of your healing is learning to own your own space, shine your light and speak with your own voice. All those fine clichés are absolutely true. Plus, there are massive satisfactions to be had, all along the way, as you grow into your full stature. (That may well be a full stature that you don't even believe that you have, right now. You will soon start to discover that the limitations that you believe you have can fall away to reveal a much more exciting vista.)

You learned to live in the shadow of other people. That has not served you.

It takes time to transform the habits of a lifetime. Time and kindness towards yourself. *"The Woman You Want To Be"* is designed to instil into you healthy habits of relating lovingly to yourself . That will happen spontaneously and incrementally as you work through the book.

You will not be asked to *"think positive"* or step so far outside your comfort zone that it could send you into panic mode. All that you need to do is tiptoe through a series of small steps that will take you on an immensely rewarding journey back to the amazing woman that you really are.

Alongside all the fear that is the legacy of a toxic relationship, somewhere deep inside, you have an aspiration about how you would like to be. This book will propel you forward, gently. Safely. At times, almost imperceptibly.

The mistake too many women make when they work on their recovery, is trying to transform their reality from the outside in. Theoretically, that makes perfect sense. First, change the outside world to look the way you would like it to, then – if you need to - sort yourself out. Unfortunately, the theory, fails to take into account the way that you work. (Not to mention the fact that it keeps you in the old pattern of putting yourself at the very bottom of your list of priorities.)

Right now, you are programmed for safety. You are not in the right state to go big, put yourself out there and run the risk of making mistakes.

So, you need to start that transformation from the inside out. If you could just go in and retool your brain overnight, I'm sure you would. (I'm sure I would have done, given half a chance.) Hell, why march through the difficult bits if you can just get to the finish line FAST? Unfortunately, that option is not currently available. That leaves you no choice but to heal and transform yourself from the inside out.

Your brain, your fears and your feelings all need to be treated with respect. They need to be given the reassurance they need. When you do that, you won't have to fight with them to change them. Instead, they will change all by themselves.

That is what happens when you work on your recovery from the inside out. You don't feel under the same level of attack (that includes self-attack) and thus you become free to shed the damaging feelings and grow.

How will you know that this is happening?

Quite simply, you will spend more of the time feeling better about yourself. Simple as that.

You will spend more time feeling happy. Plus, you will notice that you feel less tormented by old fears and more able to handle situations you previously found threatening. You will get more joy out of your day.

I know how hard it has been for you to get to the point where you are now. So, I would like to share with you these important truths as you start this journey.

You are not so broken that you cannot put yourself back together and be a more beautiful, resilient version of yourself. You are far stronger than you believe.

You will meet someone along the way for whom you will have a deep regard – your true self.

You will do far better in the life that lies ahead of you than you could imagine. Because you will –finally - own your amazing self.

So, go head and get started. You will do really well.

Warm wishes for your healing and happiness,

Annie

P.S. Please feel free to share your progress and your wins with me. Just drop me an email.

If at any time you feel you would more support working through a specific issue that comes up, then you might benefit from some individual coaching.

Once again, just send me an email to:

annie@recoverfromemotionalabuse.com

Chapter 1

Only Invest...

When you were a child, did you have a piggy bank? Did you save up your coins so that one day you could open the piggy bank up, take out all your dimes and spend them all in one fell swoop? Worse, did you have one of those piggy banks that you had to smash before you could get to the money you'd saved? Or were you one of those kids who spent every dime you had straight away, on something you "just couldn't live without"?

Either way, there tends to be something a little depressing about saving: it's the old "You get out what you put in" stuff, the subtext being, "There are no miracles, just a finite amount of money, good fortune, etc." Saving may be a good thing to do, but it certainly isn't sexy. You don't hear people getting excited about it.

But how about this? Every coin, as you know, has two sides. From where I'm standing, the other side of the coin of saving is compound interest, which is when every dime you save just keeps on multiplying. In financial circles, compound interest has been termed "The 8th wonder of the world." Are you willing to invest in the 8th wonder of the world?

If someone were to offer you either $1,000 a day for 30 days or 1 cent on day 1, 2 cents on day 2, 4 cents on day 3, doubling the amount for 30 days, which would you take? If you opt for the $30,000, perhaps you're coming out of a scarcity mentality and can't see that the dimes could amount to much.

In fact, over 30 days they would become $10,737,418.23

How does that relate to changing your life?

From today on, I am asking you to make an ongoing investment in yourself, by which I mean a real investment; not in your hair, makeup, clothes, going to the gym—all of which is largely window dressing. Nor do I mean taking up yoga, doing a computer course, learning a new skill, eating more healthily. All these are excellent things to do and you deserve to be praised for doing them. But what concerns me is that you can do all of these things and still not uproot the underlying negative beliefs that blight your life.

The ongoing investment in yourself that I am asking you to make is about planting the seeds of positive beliefs about yourself in your mind. Contrary to what you may think, positive beliefs are pretty sturdy things: you won't have to work at weeding out all the old beliefs and get the terrain ready before you can plant the new ones. You only have to get the new ones into the soil and water them daily for a period of time and they'll do the job for you. Like bindweed they will grow at a rate of knots, overrunning the old plants and, in due course, choking them to death.

It's that simple. You have only to commit to seeing yourself in this new, positive light for the miracle of compounding interest to start to work for you. I'm not suggesting that as of today—or at the latest tomorrow—you will suddenly have an entirely different outlook on life. But if you are willing to do the work of taking hold of a positive vision, even if that vision is a few steps ahead of where you feel you are, then you will start to develop a new attitude to life, and to yourself.

In terms of the returns you will get, the commitment of your time and energy is modest in the extreme: maybe 15 minutes a day.

What your investment will produce will be a compounding yield of optimism, confidence, self-worth, faith, joy, fearlessness, creativity, and connection with other people.

Given that those are the rewards, are you prepared to make a 15-minute commitment, daily, over the next year? If you're not, that's fine because it is an accurate reflection of your current emotional state and hesitancy regarding change. But if you're not prepared to make that commitment, would you at least pick up pen and paper and spend 15 minutes, just once, writing down why you're not, so that you can be clear about what is holding you back?

If you are willing, then now is the time to enter into a binding contract with yourself; no more putting things off until you feel better, or have more time, less problems, or less on your mind. That might be a long time coming. Instead of making these things pre-conditions, put them on hold for just a tiny fraction of your day while you invest in yourself, and watch them come about as results of your investment.

The First Step

Without further delay, get your pen and paper and write out your contract with yourself.

Write out:

- The date:
- Your name:
- The main emotions in your world now:
- The main emotions you want in your world one year from now:

Now write:

I hereby contract to invest **15 minutes a day** in my own spiritual and emotional growth over the next year.

I will let nothing stop me from honoring this contract except serious illness.

I hereby contract to nurture a new vision of my place in the world:

From this day on, I will invest in myself.

From this day on, I acknowledge that I am precious.

From this day on, I will honor myself.

From this day on, I will be respectful of my feelings.

From this day on, I will be careful of myself.

From this day on, I will nurture myself.

From this day on, I will cherish myself.

From this day on, I will take charge of my thoughts.

From this day on, I allow my soul to grow.

From this day on, good things will find me.

From this day on, the courage I need will be given to me.

From this day on, my strength and my optimism will grow.

From this day on, I become a role model for women and children everywhere who suffer as I suffered.

You can now sign your contract and put it somewhere safe.

Congratulations. You have just taken the first step back down the road to wholeness.

Chapter 2

The Path to Self-Recovery

Are you wondering where you go from here?

Are you asking yourself how it all works? Or are you just really keen to get started and experience a different way of being?

Be careful, now. Take a good look at the kind of expectations that you are entertaining at this point. You need to know what your expectations are. If they are not met quite quickly, you are liable to feel disappointed. You might be tempted to question the value of what you are doing.

But what is there to tell you your expectations are helpful? How often do they spur you on, and how often do they discourage you? How often have your expectations been met?

Have you thought that your expectations may well be limiting you?

Your expectations may well be narrowing your vision so that you fail to register opportunities, feedback, and evidence that could serve you. If you walk along a street with your head down, you could miss seeing a beautiful sky, a tree in bud, a passer-by whose smile would brighten your mood. If the opinionated little voice of expectation is whispering in your ear, *"If it doesn't look like this, then it's of no value,"* how many possible opportunities and pleasures has it caused to slip by unnoticed?

There has never been a better time to challenge this persistent little voice than the present. Ask yourself, *"Where do my expectations come from? Who or what informed them?"* Maybe you're not too clear about that—in which case it could be time for you to start viewing them a little more critically.

Right now, though, you're going to offer them a little guidance; you're going to notify them that you are setting out on a journey and if they want to accompany you they will have to be open to new ideas and new experiences.

The journey will be quite a long and exciting one and you will want to get as much out of it as you can, so you won't just be focusing on your destination; you have set your intention to enjoy all the sights along the way. Sometimes, on a journey, people lose track of time and they lose sight of the ground they have covered and the sights they have seen, so you will make a conscious effort to record both. You can't afford to rely on expectation, because expectation can be a lazy and unreliable chronicler.

If what you have experienced doesn't match the one outcome expectation is looking for, it might say, *"Nothing much happened,"* even when something as major as a sea change occurred. Or if you experience a lot of minor but significant shifts, they may just be disregarded if they don't fit with expectation's mood. Expectation never asks itself, *"Am I missing something?"* So, on this journey, you will be the guide and you will set your direction in accordance with the new insights and beliefs you acquire along the way.

As the journey is going to last nearly a year, you won't be wanting to set out on it with too much baggage to weigh you down. You'll want to travel as light as you can. As the journey goes on, you'll be surprised to realize how much excess baggage you used to carry around and how much better you feel without it. Your journey will be divided into a number of steps; at each one you will be provided with all the kit you need.

With Step One, you contracted to invest in yourself.

From now on, each chapter of this book will contain a numbered Step. Each Step will be a stage of your journey. The fifteen minutes a day you contracted to invest in yourself will be spent reading the numbered Step, three times a day, from Monday to Friday for five weeks. You will read the Step for the first time each morning on waking, for the second time in the middle of the day, at a set point—say, after you have had your lunch. The final time, when you go to bed, you will read out loud.

Your other commitment will be to fill in the **Journey Recorder** that follows each Step, nightly. You will be requested to fill in the date, the number of times you have read the Step, and also to review the brief paragraph and assess how you have fared in applying it each day.

You will **rate yourself** on a scale of 1- 4.

- 1 is fair,
- 2 good,
- 3 very good,
- 4 outstanding.

This is an important part of the process. If you are in doubt about how to rate yourself, bearing in mind your habit of self-criticism, go ahead and rate yourself one point above your initial self-judgment.

That's all there is to it. Except in the case of serious illness or annual holidays, you will read each Step three times a day. If, for either reason, you should have to interrupt the contract, you will start again where you left off on the first Monday when you are back in your routine.

Is that enough to change your life's direction?

Yes, it is. By reading each Step three times a day for five weeks, you are planting and watering vigorous seeds which will put down strong roots in both your conscious mind and your subconscious mind. The growth these seedlings make will confound your habitual (aka old) expectations, but you can deal with that. When the choice is between being constrained in your old life by old expectations or else having the freedom to travel to fresh horizons, there is no contest.

In *Happiness Now*, Robert Holden writes, *"Know, therefore, that the journey to true happiness and to happiness now is not a journey of physical distance or time; it is one of personal 'self-recovery,' where we remember and reconnect consciously to an inner potential for joy—a paradise lost—waiting to be found."*

That is what you will do through the steps that follow.

Chapter 3

Only Celebrate...

What do you have to celebrate today?

Maybe it's not something you would normally ask yourself. Maybe you don't think you have a great deal to celebrate. It all depends on your perspective.

If I asked you what you have to feel sad, anxious, or aggrieved about in your life, you could probably reel off quite a list. But I don't want to hear it and you don't need to hear it anymore. Whatever has happened has happened, and it has blighted enough of your life.

My not wanting to hear about it is not about not caring. In fact I care very much. But I've been there myself. Twenty-seven years in an abusive marriage left me feeling so ashamed, so frightened, drained, humiliated, isolated, and worthless that I took refuge in these feelings. I felt that I had had it so bad that nobody could understand me. I also felt that joy and self-worth were only available to other people who had not experienced this endless erosion of their being.

I was wrong on both counts. I discovered that any number of women had been through what I had and worse. Not that it is ever a competition. Whatever agony each of us endures is agony enough. I discovered also that I had no power to change past miseries, but that I can choose my perspective, moment by moment, and day by day.

So let me ask you again: What do you have to celebrate today?

Often when people are first faced with this question, they find it difficult to respond. On this first occasion may I prompt you, just so that you can be sure you get the general idea? Let's say that I'm showing you the rules of a new game.

You see, I believe you have a number of things to celebrate today, which include:

- Your **resilience**, despite all that you have been through.
- Your **courage**, in committing to this new course despite your fears.
- Your **faith**, because you are prepared to confront your doubts.
- Your **vitality**, because in the end you refuse to give up.
- Your **honesty**, because you are willing to own the reality of your situation.
- Your **caring**, because even when you were too low to care for yourself, you still cared for others.
- Your **wisdom**, because owning your own truth is the source of all wisdom.
- The **gift** of this day that you can color with joy, sorrow, anger, or whatever emotion you choose.
- The **future** that still lies ahead of you.
- Your **survival**.

I Am a Survivor

There was a woman who had long lived alone and she hungered for the love that would light up her life. In the fullness of time, a man appeared who spoke to her of love and held her in his arms the way she had always dreamed, and she knew him as the love of her life. So the woman gave the man her heart, her mind, and her life. She put none above him or level with him—least of all herself. None could compare with him. Often she said that she would give all that she had, and gladly, for just one day of the bliss she had known since she became his.

But bliss is at best a fleeting state and marital bliss can vanish with the first rays of the morning sun. The lovers did not know how to reconcile their extraordinary, all-consuming love with ordinary life. They did not know the susceptibility of even the strongest passion. Still less did they know how powerfully routine could erode the fragile foundations of their precious citadel.

They could not safeguard the treasure that was theirs because they knew naught of its weaknesses and their own frailties. They had not the skills to protect their dwelling place. Nor had they the wherewithal to defend each other and themselves from the assault of prosaic reality. Increasingly, as they saw the outermost walls of the citadel crumble away at their touch, they become disillusioned with themselves, with each other, and with the edifice that they had merely inhabited, never thinking how they might preserve it.

The woman increasingly sought to reassure herself and her husband, saying, "Even if the east wing has gone, still all these rooms remain. These rooms will be enough for us. We can make the best of what we have." But the man saw only an edifice that was disintegrating and began to wish he was free of it, for what kind of man was he that could not inhabit his dream?

Worse, he knew that weakness and distress were frowned upon in that land and he feared that he might come to be shunned. So anxious was he not to lose face that, almost without thinking about it, he began looking about for another love with whom he could rebuild his dreams. Nor was he long in finding one.

He held on to the old until he had assured himself that his new love would better meet his needs. Only then did he tell his wife that he had long been dissatisfied and was leaving her that day.

The woman, who had learned how to accept an ever-shrinking share of happiness, was devastated. If her husband forced her to abandon the crumbling edifice they had shared, destitution awaited her. She would have been grateful to share even the dilapidated stable with him. She tried, in vain, to persuade her husband to value what they had had, what she felt they might still have, but the ruined citadel held no charms for him now that he could once more dwell in a palace.

He left the woman crouched in the rubble of the ruined citadel, too terrified to move. For days she lay face down on its broken floor, too afraid to raise her head, with no thought of hunger or thirst, deprived of even the release of sleep. She prayed for the floor to split open so that the earth might swallow her. She longed for the swift release of death but it was denied her.

At length she was forced to respond to the demands of her aching, starving body and she resigned herself to living. She resolved to drag herself through the endless, desolate night of his absence until her body should finally fail her, and she yearned for that moment when she could lay down the agony of her loneliness. Abandoned by the husband she had so loved and revered, she had given up on life.

But life did not give up on her. It lay in wait for her with an infinity of small joys throughout that time of grievous hardship, and their profusion was such that even she could not be blind to them.

So it was that the woman learned to cherish life for its own sake. She learned that the altar of romantic love, where she had previously worshipped, was but the altar of a jealous, exclusive idol. She learned that there were many kinds of love, and all were precious; all nurtured her soul. She learned to cherish the myriad gifts that each day brings to those who will see them.

And she rejoiced that she had been restored to life.

Step 2

I AM A SURVIVOR, AND FROM THIS DAY ON I WILL CELEBRATE ALL THE BLESSINGS THAT ARE MINE.

No more am I a victim of past circumstances; I am a survivor with the wisdom and resources that only survivors have. When I look back along the path I have travelled, I see the obstacles, pits, and hurdles that have punctuated my journey.

From today I make the choice to focus not on the hardships of the past but the strengths that have enabled me to persist and overcome.

I see now that I chose not to surrender to the difficulties that crowded in on me. Even in my darkest hours I chose love and support for those who are dearest to me. Despite the magnitude of the struggle, again and again I chose life and love over despair. When I could not entertain that vision for myself, I still clung to it for those around me.

I AM A SURVIVOR, AND FROM THIS DAY ON I WILL CELEBRATE ALL THE BLESSINGS THAT ARE MINE.

As I kept hold, with love, of a vision for others, so now will I hold a vision for myself. From this day on, I nurture the vision of my strengths. I acknowledge the courage and endurance that enabled me to persist despite my sense of futility and hopelessness. I own and give thanks for my fortitude. Despite a sense of worthlessness and pointlessness that often came close to overwhelming me, I did not allow myself to be crushed.

Henceforth I will keep in my mind the thought that, notwithstanding my sense of powerlessness, I did battle, daily, with despair. I will remember that, however great the odds, however many times I was cast down and wounded by people and events, I have always returned to the fray and fought, with whatever strength I had, for my faith in life and in myself.

I have been sorely tested yet I have won out.

I AM A SURVIVOR, AND FROM THIS DAY ON I WILL CELEBRATE THE BLESSINGS THAT ARE MINE.

As I have loved others with a fierce, protective love, so now will I love myself. From this day on, I will protect my well-being as jealously as ever a lioness protects her cubs. In the past I have always freely offered my love, care, and support to those who have suffered and were in need; now I will extend the same love and care to myself also.

As I have trusted that others can heal, so do I trust in my healing. As I have trusted in the power of my love to help others to heal, so now do I trust that I have love enough and power enough to heal myself.

I AM A SURVIVOR, AND FROM THIS DAY ON I WILL CELEBRATE ALL THE BLESSINGS THAT ARE MINE.

My past is a mine from which I can extract the precious materials that will provide me with future abundance. As I review my past, I begin to make sense of the gifts it offers, the lessons to be learned from my mistakes and frailties. There is no shame in owning the failings and frailties of the past. Rather, they are to be embraced. It is only by accepting them that I become free to focus on my qualities, to uncover my vision, to nurture my dreams. As I warm to the human frailties of others, now I will regard with affection my own also. No longer will I mask my need for support and affection with the semblance of the woman too proud, too strong, and too aloof to seek help, which served only to compound my isolation.

I AM A SURVIVOR, AND FROM THIS DAY ON I WILL CELEBRATE ALL THE BLESSINGS THAT ARE MINE.

I am the architect of my future and my present. My future may yet look modest and uncertain because I had ceased even to lay claim to a future of my own, yet I am laying a firm foundation by my acknowledgement of present strengths and my openness to future possibilities. For now my future may look as modest as a single-room dwelling, but the space and materials available to me are unlimited. As I expand—and I will expand—so too will my future.

I AM A SURVIVOR, AND FROM THIS DAY ON I WILL CELEBRATE ALL THE BLESSINGS THAT ARE MINE.

No edifice is constructed in one day. Before foundations can be laid, the ground must first be torn up. The first stages of construction give little sign of the creative vision of the architect and builder. But with a good plan, the right materials, and the strength and skills of those who build it, it becomes a beautiful, harmonious creation. I am clarifying my plans, gathering my materials and enlisting the strength and skills required. The edifice that I build now will be beautiful, spacious, and enduring.

I give thanks for the opportunity that has been given to me and I will use it to the fullest.

I AM A SURVIVOR, AND FROM THIS DAY ON I WILL CELEBRATE ALL THE BLESSINGS THAT ARE MINE.

No more will my life be a never-ending succession of thankless labors. No more will I look forward to a present and future of hardship and ceaseless toil. Instead I will rejoice in my own abundant energy, my appetite for work and for life that has allowed me to survive such a world of difficulties and toil.

I AM A SURVIVOR, AND FROM THIS DAY ON I WILL CELEBRATE ALL THE BLESSINGS THAT ARE MINE.

From today I view the universe with different eyes. No more will I focus on hardship and toil, although they may yet be with me a while. Instead I will focus on all the miracles of life—the small even more than the great. For while it is not given to us to enjoy great miracles daily, to each of us each day there are presented many tiny miracles if we will but see them. Henceforth I will acknowledge each ray of light that shines into my life; every act of kindness; every word of friendship; every promise and sign of positive change; each opportunity, however small, that comes my way. For I know that there is no more powerful way of driving hardship and sorrow from my life than offering a prayer of acknowledgement and gratitude for all those gifts that previously passed unnoticed.

I AM A SURVIVOR, AND FROM THIS DAY ON I WILL CELEBRATE ALL THE BLESSINGS THAT ARE MINE.

From this day on, my eyes are open to the beauties of the world and they are all mine to enjoy. I will delight freely in the beauty of a flower, the majesty of a tree, the splendor of a sunset, the smile of a child, the song of a bird, the beauty of a voice, the magic of shared laughter. I will take heart from the endless sources of joy that surround me and I too will be a source of joy for others.

I AM A SURVIVOR, AND FROM THIS DAY ON I WILL CELEBRATE ALL THE BLESSINGS OF THIS WORLD THAT HAVE BEEN RESTORED TO ME.

Week 1 Recorder

I have celebrated the blessings that are mine. I have acknowledged every word of friendship and act of kindness. I have rejoiced in my own energy and my appetite for life.

Monday   DATE

Number of times the Step was read:
Your score:
Total score:

Tuesday   DATE

Number of times the Step was read:
Your score:
Total score:

Wednesday   DATE

Number of times the Step was read:
Your score:
Total score:

THURSDAY   DATE

Number of times the Step was read:

Your score:

Total score:

FRIDAY   DATE

Number of times the Step was read:

Your score:

Total score:

Your end of week score:

QUOTATION

You feel most relevant to yourself this week:

_____
_____
_____
_____
_____
_____
_____
_____

Your achievements of the week:

_____
_____
_____
_____
_____
_____
_____
_____

Week 2 Recorder

I have celebrated the blessings that are mine. I have acknowledged every word of friendship and act of kindness. I have rejoiced in my own energy and my appetite for life.

Monday   Date

Number of times the Step was read:
Your score:
Total score:

Tuesday   Date

Number of times the Step was read:
Your score:
Total score:

Wednesday   Date

Number of times the Step was read:
Your score:
Total score:

THURSDAY   DATE

Number of times the Step was read:

Your score:

Total score:

FRIDAY   DATE

Number of times the Step was read:

Your score:

Total score:

Your end of week score:

QUOTATION

You feel most relevant to yourself this week:

_____
_____
_____
_____
_____
_____
_____
_____

Your achievements of the week:

_____
_____
_____
_____
_____
_____
_____
_____

Week 3 Recorder

I have celebrated the blessings that are mine. I have acknowledged every word of friendship and act of kindness. I have rejoiced in my own energy and my appetite for life.

MONDAY   DATE

Number of times the Step was read:
Your score:
Total score:

TUESDAY   DATE

Number of times the Step was read:
Your score:
Total score:

WEDNESDAY   DATE

Number of times the Step was read:
Your score:
Total score:

THURSDAY   DATE

Number of times the Step was read:

Your score:

Total score:

FRIDAY   DATE

Number of times the Step was read:

Your score:

Total score:

Your end of week score:

QUOTATION

You feel most relevant to yourself this week:

_____
_____
_____
_____
_____
_____
_____
_____

Your achievements of the week:

_____
_____
_____
_____
_____
_____
_____
_____
_____

Week 4 Recorder

I have celebrated the blessings that are mine. I have acknowledged every word of friendship and act of kindness. I have rejoiced in my own energy and my appetite for life.

Monday   Date

Number of times the Step was read:
Your score:
Total score:

Tuesday   Date

Number of times the Step was read:
Your score:
Total score:

Wednesday   Date

Number of times the Step was read:
Your score:
Total score:

THURSDAY   DATE

Number of times the Step was read:

Your score:

Total score:

FRIDAY   DATE

Number of times the Step was read:

Your score:

Total score:

Your end of week score:

Quotation

You feel most relevant to yourself this week:

_____

_____

_____

_____

_____

_____

_____

_____

Your achievements of the week:
_____
_____
_____
_____
_____
_____
_____
_____

Week 5 Recorder

I have celebrated the blessings that are mine. I have acknowledged every word of friendship and act of kindness. I have rejoiced in my own energy and my appetite for life.

Monday   Date

Number of times the Step was read:
Your score: _____
Total score: _____
                                                       _____

Tuesday   Date

Number of times the Step was read:
Your score: _____
Total score: _____
                                                       _____

Wednesday   Date

Number of times the Step was read:
Your score: _____
Total score: _____
                                                       _____

THURSDAY   DATE

Number of times the Step was read:

Your score:

Total score:

FRIDAY   DATE

Number of times the Step was read:

Your score:

Total score:

Your end of week score:

QUOTATION

You feel most relevant to yourself this week:

_____
_____
_____
_____
_____
_____
_____
_____

Your achievements of the week:

_____
_____
_____
_____
_____
_____
_____
_____

Chapter 4

Only See...

Five weeks have passed. Five weeks of committed, consistent investment in yourself. I'd like to commend you for that; you have laid a firm foundation for your future growth, even though you may have found it hard work at times.

But more than that I'd like you to commend yourself. I'd like you to register what an enormous step forward you have taken.

Chaim Potok wrote, *"All beginnings are hard."* When a new beginning requires you to challenge old thinking, uproot ingrained habits and also acquire momentum, it's no wonder it's hard. Inertia would place far fewer demands on you, apparently. Although, in reality, you'd be struggling to stay afloat in a sea of molasses—and the effort required of you, which is probably all too familiar to you, would be huge.

But you have taken the decision to swim, not just to tread water. You have chosen to see yourself in a new light. It's not so much the facts as your mindset that makes you a survivor. As such, you belong to a very special group; you belong to that group of people whose soul will not be crushed or maimed by their past experiences. You belong to that fortunate group whose past sufferings teach them to savor the moment. Already you are traveling to a place of peace, beyond the regrets, recriminations and despair that had ensnared you.

Henceforward, you are the architect of your own life.

You can design and construct that life in the place and the style that you choose, provided you continue to invest time, trust, and patience. Rabbi Pinchas said, *"What you pursue, you don't get. But what you allow to grow slowly in its own way, comes to you."* The architect in you is currently sketching out the first draft of your future plans; the fledgling survivor in you is only starting to become aware of your possibilities.

Arthur Schopenhauer observed, *"Everyone takes the limits of his own vision for the limits of the world."* Time, then, to explore beyond the old limits that curtailed your vision.

My Spirit is Free to Soar

Once upon a time, there was a baby who was born into a cage. The child's parents put the child into a cage at birth not so much because they were cruel, but because they were afraid. They did not know how they could handle their child's potential and they felt small and frightened. For they too had been caged from birth until, in the fullness of time, the constraints of the cage had molded their very souls.

So they put their child also into a cage, where they felt that the child would be safe. And they felt that they also would be safe. The world as they knew it could continue. They had a terrible fear of chaos, of the world, their lives, everything falling in on them if the bars of the cage were not there to hold it all up.

So their child grew up in a cage. She grew and grew. The space available to the child became smaller and smaller with each month that passed and the child adapted increasingly to the constraints of the cage. The parents observed her development through the bars of the cage and they were reassured. They felt that all was as right as it could be with their world.

There would be no risk that their child would prick her finger on a spindle and die. There would be no risk of their child encountering the big, bad wolf. No risk of their child traveling to the ends of the earth and leaving them behind. There would be no risk of their child ever breaking out of the cage, expanding into the unknown and dwarfing them. No risk of their child ever turning away from them and rejecting their world. No risk of the child confronting the dangers and excitement that lurked outside the cage—as they had not— and leaving them feeling small and powerless.

So the child continued to grow and the parents continued to see that the child received the sustenance it was possible to receive through the bars of a cage. They ensured that the child had friends who also lived in cages. They taught the child that, to be a good person, the child had to live in a cage. Only cage dwellers were decent human beings.

Within the cage the child grew and grew. Daily she folded herself up smaller so as not to be pressing up against the bars of the cage. She hunched herself into the most compact shape she could to win her parents' approval. Yet the child sensed that there was a world rich with possibilities beyond the bars of the cage; a world that was only available to those of a different race. And a sense of loss set in, together with a sense of worthlessness. The child started to will herself smaller, and the parents rejoiced. Their education was working. The child would be safe —and so would they. The time-honored order would continue throughout the generations.

But the child could not still her longing for life outside the cage. Despite the fear and the deprivation and the doubt and the worthlessness, the child longed for more. One thing that her parents had not spoken of, for they knew it not, was the power of longing.

The child remained many years in that cage in sorrow and in longing. The sorrow was such that the child did not even raise her head enough to notice what the power of longing had brought about. But so great was the power of longing that it had caused the door of the cage to open.

Now, that door remained open for a long time, and every so often harbingers of the outside world made their way in. The child, who was a child no more, would examine them without question. The child-woman did not dare even to ask, "How has this thing made its way into my cage?" But the door of the cage remained open and soon small creatures too strayed in and left. Once or twice a person also stepped in and tried to coax the child-woman out.

The person saw before them someone with the body of an adult and they would speak to the adult and urge her to step out of the cage. Sometimes the child-adult would want to very much, but in the end she could not. In the end it was always the child that spoke through the adult's lips and refused. The prospect was too frightening, for the child-adult was not ready.

Yet in the loneliness and discomfort of the cage, the child-woman was slowly, unconsciously gathering evidence about what lay outside. She became aware that outside lay not simply chaos but a complex world populated by good people as well as demons; a world in which destruction and cruelty were not certainties. And the longing grew ever greater.

She began to spend more and more time gazing through the open door of the cage. The parents, who lacked the power to close it again, watched in fear and told her repeatedly how safe she was, how protected, how wild animals waited beyond the bars to tear her apart. The child-woman did not doubt that this would be her lot. She accepted that it would be as her parents had said: she could remain in safety within the confines of her cage where the life would surely be crushed out of her; or else she could be torn apart even as she struggled to free herself.

But the child-woman could not help herself. She was driven by a life force too powerful to deny. With much pain and fear and hesitation she eventually struggled through the open door of the cage and got to her feet to wait for the destruction, which she knew must surely be imminent.

There she stood for a long time, too terrified to move. While she stood there, fierce animals passed her. Some snarled at her and departed; others harmed her, often the same animal returning to harm her repeatedly. But people came along too who offered her their hand and sought to support her and help her explore her freedom.

For a long time she could not accept. She dare not trust and dare not move, so there she stood, rooted to the spot, paralyzed by fear. And always in the background she heard the voices of her parents ordering her back into her cage.

Sometimes it was only those voices that enabled her to endure, that reminded her that the agony of her prison was greater than the agony of this fearful freedom.

But the child-woman grew wise. She realized that the onslaught of fierce animals could hurt her and cow her, but it had not broken her. She became aware of her endurance, if not her strength and her power, and she began, at last, to accept herself. She was not merely a caged child; she was a woman capable of making choices for herself, capable of creating and shaping her own existence.

She realized at length that as she had done, so could she do. She had stepped out of her cage. She had dared to shape her own existence and she had survived. Now she would commit her energies to shaping her life into a house of many rooms. In the interests not just of herself but her children and her children's children, down through the generations, she would fashion a life of beauty and space in a dwelling place of her own choosing.

She told herself how hard it would be. She anticipated a struggle beyond any that she had encountered before. She resigned herself to setbacks and suffering, because that was all she had ever been taught to expect and because she was still blind to her own gifts, her own strength, the miracle of her being.

Along the way, she made many discoveries. She discovered that she had already completed the hardest part of the journey; that there was much support around her that she could call upon; that the joys far outweighed the sorrows; that she had many more qualities, talents and resources than ever she would have believed. She discovered also that she was admirable and an inspiration to others; that she had no need to struggle alone; that she had wings to fly, if only she would.

Step 3

My spirit is free to soar.

No longer will other people's expectations hem me in. No more will I resign myself to be caged by my past experience, tethered by the demands of others, blinkered by their anxieties.

My spirit is free to soar.

My life and my spirit have no need to be earthbound. I am not a worm that crawls through the soil without ever glimpsing the stars. No more will my world, like that of the worm, be limited to what lies beneath me, what lies immediately over me, bearing down on me. No more will past, present, and future stretch out drab and unyielding, arid as the sun- parched clay. No more will I struggle for survival in a harsh and hostile environment.

I am not a worm. I am earth-born but not earthbound. From today I will soar above that life of futile drabness.

My spirit is free to soar.

The constraints of the past served not to protect me but only to limit me and I now throw them off; for I trust that I possess the wisdom and the resources to protect myself. From this day on, I cast off the shackles that bound me, denying me the freedom to change and grow at will. I will not hang back for fear of the dangers that may lie ahead. No longer do they have the power to crush me, for now I see that they are but tests of my mettle and I rise above them.

No longer can the past hold me hostage, for I have within me a well-spring of courage and wisdom that enables me to step, trusting, into the future.

I am not a worm. I do not live at the mercy of any creature that would prey on me. I am a songbird and I choose to fly.

My spirit is free to soar.

For too long my wings were folded and untried. Only now do I start to spread and test them. The first flights may be brief, until I get the measure of my powers, but my spirit yearns for the unbounded vistas that await me. As I take to the wing, leaving the ground beneath me, my vision encompasses the vast sweep of the landscape–and its beauty dazzles me.

I choose my habitation and my resting place. I can roam over forests and lakes; I can explore fields, lowlands, rugged coastlines, hills, and mountain peaks–for now I have wings to fly.

My spirit is free to soar.

From this moment on, I choose my companions from creatures of my own species: other birds, whose song delights by its beauty and purity. The higher I soar, the more beautiful my song becomes. It gives joy and hope to those below. My song fills me too with wonder for I well remember how, in my earthbound days, I could utter only a tuneless lament. My song is an ode to the sanctity of life, the infinite possibility of rebirth, the indestructibility of the human spirit.

My spirit is free to soar.

From my vantage point above the clouds, I see all that I have achieved even from within the confines of my prison. I see also that I am free to live my dreams and be productive beyond my wildest imaginings.

I give thanks for all the blessings I have received and the many blessings I know await me. I rejoice in the gifts that have been bestowed upon me: the gift of flight that enables me to soar above cares and troubles; the gift of song through which I give expression to my unique voice and offer pleasure and comfort even to those who know me not.

My spirit is free to soar.

No longer will I hold myself in check. No more will I squander my energies by doubting or turning my back on my talents. Henceforth I will celebrate my uniqueness. My time to take flight has come. I embrace my potential, I cherish my sensibilities, I acknowledge my flair. I give free rein to my abilities. As I nurture my gifts, so do they multiply.

My spirit is free to soar.

Now I begin anew each day, open to all the promise that it brings. No longer do I fear difficulties, for they will only sharpen my resolve. The challenges along my way I now welcome, for they stimulate me to ever greater achievement. The obstacles on my path I greet as gifts, for I have wings to rise above them, and the higher I fly the more do new opportunities open up before me. The problems I encounter serve only to reveal the extent of my powers.

My spirit is free to soar and I give thanks with outstretched wings.

Week 6 Recorder

I have rejoiced in the gifts that have been bestowed on me and I have started to test and spread my wings.

MONDAY   DATE

Number of times the Step was read:
Your score:
Total score:

TUESDAY   DATE

Number of times the Step was read:
Your score:
Total score:

WEDNESDAY   DATE

Number of times the Step was read:
Your score:
Total score:

THURSDAY   DATE

Number of times the Step was read:

Your score:

Total score:

FRIDAY   DATE

Number of times the Step was read:

Your score:

Total score:

Your end of week score:

QUOTATION

You feel most relevant to yourself this week:

_____
_____
_____
_____
_____
_____
_____
_____

Your achievements of the week:

_____
_____
_____
_____
_____
_____
_____
_____

Week 7 Recorder

I have rejoiced in the gifts that have been bestowed on me and I have started to test and spread my wings.

MONDAY   DATE

Number of times the Step was read:
Your score:
Total score:

TUESDAY   DATE

Number of times the Step was read:
Your score:
Total score:

WEDNESDAY   DATE

Number of times the Step was read:
Your score:
Total score:

THURSDAY   DATE

Number of times the Step was read:

Your score:

Total score:

FRIDAY   DATE

Number of times the Step was read:

Your score:

Total score:

Your end of week score:

QUOTATION

You feel most relevant to yourself this week:

_____
_____
_____
_____
_____
_____
_____
_____

Your achievements of the week:
_____
_____
_____
_____
_____
_____
_____
_____

Week 8 Recorder

I have rejoiced in the gifts that have been bestowed on me and I have started to test and spread my wings.

Monday   Date

Number of times the Step was read:
Your score:
Total score:

Tuesday   Date

Number of times the Step was read:
Your score:
Total score:

Wednesday   Date

Number of times the Step was read:
Your score:
Total score:

THURSDAY   DATE

Number of times the Step was read:
Your score:
Total score:

FRIDAY   DATE

Number of times the Step was read:
Your score:
Total score:

Your end of week score:

QUOTATION

You feel most relevant to yourself this week:

_____
_____
_____
_____
_____
_____
_____
_____

Your achievements of the week:

_____
_____
_____
_____
_____
_____
_____
_____

Week 9 Recorder

I have rejoiced in the gifts that have been bestowed on me and I have started to test and spread my wings.

MONDAY   DATE

Number of times the Step was read: _____
Your score: _____
Total score: _____

TUESDAY   DATE

Number of times the Step was read: _____
Your score: _____
Total score: _____

WEDNESDAY   DATE

Number of times the Step was read: _____
Your score: _____
Total score: _____

THURSDAY   DATE

Number of times the Step was read:

Your score:

Total score:

FRIDAY   DATE

Number of times the Step was read:

Your score:

Total score:

Your end of week score:

QUOTATION

You feel most relevant to yourself this week:

_____
_____
_____
_____
_____
_____
_____
_____

Your achievements of the week:

_____
_____
_____
_____
_____
_____
_____
_____

Week 10 Recorder

I have rejoiced in the gifts that have been bestowed on me and I have started to test and spread my wings.

MONDAY   DATE

Number of times the Step was read:
Your score:
Total score:

TUESDAY   DATE

Number of times the Step was read:
Your score:
Total score:

WEDNESDAY   DATE

Number of times the Step was read:
Your score:
Total score:

THURSDAY   DATE

Number of times the Step was read:

Your score:

Total score:

FRIDAY   DATE

Number of times the Step was read:

Your score:

Total score:

Your end of week score:

QUOTATION

You feel most relevant to yourself this week:

_____
_____
_____
_____
_____
_____
_____
_____

Your achievements of the week:
_____
_____
_____
_____
_____
_____
_____
_____

Chapter 5

You Are Your Voice

Do you ever feel blocked by the things you achieved in the past?

Do you find yourself thinking that you don't measure up to the image of the woman you were before? Have you been paralyzed by the fear that you won't be good enough in the future?

We call it *"self-talk,"* but whose voice is it that you hear when these thoughts are going through your brain?

You see, I don't believe for one moment that that voice is yours. What I believe is that at some point in your life you have heard that voice—or those voices—until your own voice was quite drowned out. You were taught, doubtless, to show care and respect, love and deference—but only to other people, chiefly a quite specific group of people. You were never taught to show love, care, and respect for yourself. You were taught to disregard yourself. And with that your voice fell silent.

Of course, that may not be quite the way it felt to you; you may have lost track of the way the process came about. But if you've ever found yourself thinking, *"It's only me"*; *"I really don't have any strong feelings about…"*; *"X is so much more knowledgeable than me"*; *"Y is so much clearer, brighter, more articulate…"* that is because your voice has been silenced for so long. No one can express your unique message. Your truth and your voice are just as valuable as anyone else's can ever be.

Do you remember the old adage, *"Stick and stones may break my bones, but words can never hurt me?"* That must be one of the most pernicious and misleading little proverbs ever coined;

words—and silence—do cause as much hurt as sticks and stones. Yet you hear this proverb in the mouths of the brutalized and it is used to justify brutalization.

The power of words is limitless.

The power of your words to affect your own self-recovery is limitless also. There is a part of you that has lain dormant through the silence that was imposed on you; it is the timeless, enduring, impregnable part of you, the essence of what is best and most charismatic about you. It is your unique birthright and it will always be there for you. The way to access it is by giving voice to it; you do so by writing and speaking your truth and your feelings in the moment.

Your being, given your experiences, is like the iceberg; some five or ten percent is visible in your habitual thinking, your daily life; the remaining ninety to ninety-five percent has been submerged by the disuse into which your voice has fallen. Now is the time to start exercising your voice and discovering your true stature.

"Never be bullied into silence. Never allow yourself to be made a victim. Accept no one's definition of your life, but define yourself."
—Anonymous.

I Have a Voice that Enriches the World

There was once a beautiful princess who grew up in a kingdom ruled by the twin tyrants of Fear and Shame. From birth, the princess was brought up to believe she was ugly, lest she disturb the long-established order. But she had a pure and generous heart, a faith in the goodness of her fellow men, a caring nature, and a touching naivety. She had a beautiful soul that shone in her eyes. Yet she believed that she was ugly and stupid and worthless. She believed that she was destined to be no more than the humble serving maid of a noble lord.

In accordance with the customs of the land, a suitor eventually presented himself. He appeared, dressed in the finery of a prince, and told the princess that she could make his life complete. She was, he said, made to be an ornament on his arm, a useful adjunct in his life.

The princess had long willed this to happen. Her education had been scant, but this thing at least she had been told: that into the life of every fortunate serving maid a prince would eventually step who would claim her for his own. Then he would kiss her and she would be his for evermore.

The suitor presented himself in the raiment of a prince, and the princess therefore believed that he was both a prince and her destiny. It was for her simply to be kissed and then walk, from that day on, in the shadow of her prince. She was to do his bidding, bear his children, and put him before her in sickness and in health, through good times and bad, for as long as he so willed it.

Now, the truth was that somewhere deep in her heart, the princess had dreamed of a suitor who would cherish her as much as life itself, but all the teachings of the kingdom had taught her that that was merely a fairy tale. A humble serving maid such as she had no entitlement to great joy. So the princess stifled a few small regrets and resolved to love the prince. So grateful was she to be The Chosen One of any suitor that she was willing to put her life at his disposal, for there was no greater disgrace in the country than to remain Unchosen.

So relief gave rise to gratitude, and gratitude gave rise to love, and the princess duly kissed the suitor and gave her life over to his care forever.

But the suitor, though he wore the raiment of a prince, was not a prince. He was not even a frog, but a toad. Once he had kissed the princess and stolen her heart, he threw off his fine clothes and revealed all the darkness in his soul. The toad was an ugly creature indeed. He was short and squat. He grew ever more cruel and brutal and self-indulgent, and his vices, increasingly, were writ large over his coarse-featured face. The more his ugliness grew, the more did he reproach the princess for her beauty and her virtue.

What became of the princess? She suffered terribly under the blows of his tongue, his hand, his loveless heart. Yet she stayed true to the teachings of her land. Long and hard did she labor to heal him with her love. She struggled to help him become a true prince until the effort was so great that it almost drove the life from her body.

Then she lost faith in the sovereign power of love. She had long since lost all faith in herself. She espoused even his hatred of herself in the vain hope that out of her prostration would somehow be born a True Prince, just as Cinderella's fairy godmother had created fine clothing and a carriage out of base matter.

It never came to pass. Her prostration was such that she ceased gazing starward. She ceased her efforts to create an epic prince in whose great shadow she could glory. In her hunger and her despair, she began at length to glance around her, to search for crumbs to feed on and any sign that might remind her of her own humanity, her own existence.

To her amazement, she found that the wasteland where she now dwelled was inhabited by others like herself, princesses cruelly laid low by toads whose true nature they had once cunningly disguised. She saw the beauty of these other broken, ravaged princesses and her heart stirred once more within her breast. Slowly, she learned to care and be cared for; she learned to recognize the beauty in her soul; she learned that she was unique and valuable.

She learned, in that desolate place, that her life was sacred and that anywhere a princess dwells can never be a wasteland. Through the love she shared in that desolate place, she and the other princesses were reborn.

Step 4

I HAVE A VOICE THAT ENRICHES THE WORLD.

In the past I have abdicated my voice and my feelings. In my abasement and my fear, I imagined that my voice mattered not, that my words were without meaning. I ascribed wisdom to others in the same measure that I accorded mere foolishness to myself.

No longer will I demean myself because others have demeaned me. No longer will I be active in my own humiliation by censoring my words and even my thoughts.

I HAVE A VOICE THAT ENRICHES THE WORLD.

From this day on, I will treat my thoughts, my feelings, and my words with due consideration. Whether they are right or wrong is immaterial for they are expressions of my unique spirit and as such they are deserving of the utmost acceptance and respect. No error can invalidate my being, for it is human to err. Nor can I make my worth greater by striving to express opinions that others will find irreproachable, for the pursuit of perfection will only diminish my humanity. Striving for an illusion of perfection serves but to alienate me from my essence and my fellows. It is only when I cease denying my frailties and I abandon my attempts to conceal my flaws from the world that my virtues shine forth and I am most deserving of regard. When I speak my truth, simply and clearly, I share my greatest gift.

I HAVE A VOICE THAT ENRICHES THE WORLD.

No longer will I entertain vain hopes that another will give voice to the thoughts that I dare not utter aloud. No longer will I wait in silent frustration for others to guess and act upon my unvoiced wishes, for in doing so I thwart my own desires and burden others futilely. None may discharge responsibility for my well-being, save only me. If I do not treat myself with due regard, why should I imagine that another person will relieve me of the oppressive weight of my feelings of worthlessness?

For too long my thinking was that of a resentful child who blames the world for her misfortunes and wills the world to rectify them. Henceforth I will give voice to my needs and wishes, for only I can right the circumstances in my life that have gone astray, regardless of how that came about. From the rubble of my past misery, I alone can salvage the supports on which I will build a future dwelling place of unique beauty. And the labor I expend will bring rich rewards, for that edifice will be a monument for others also.

I HAVE A VOICE THAT ENRICHES THE WORLD.

Only I can step into my true stature; there is none other who can do it for me. Yet, in the past, I was fearful of fostering my merits, lest I somehow deprive others of their worth. I made myself smaller and more insignificant than ever I was, for fear of overshadowing others, almost as if it were in my power to deprive them of light and air; and in so doing, I futilely patronized them and demeaned myself. Now I see my treatment of the world is but a reflection of my treatment of myself. No more shall I diminish myself and diminish the world.

I HAVE A VOICE THAT ENRICHES THE WORLD.

Henceforth I will speak my truth, for as I am unique, so too is my truth. I will contribute its singular hue to the richly colored mosaic of this world. Henceforth I will observe how the harmonies and contrasts it creates complement that vast mosaic; and I will rejoice in the knowledge that, small as I am, my place is not insignificant and none can fill it save me. By moving into my rightful place, I make my contribution to the overall beauty of the world, and am myself greatly enhanced.

I HAVE A VOICE THAT ENRICHES THE WORLD.

From this day on, I undertake to honor my being, for it is only when I show honor to my own being that I truly honor my fellows. No longer will I attempt to conceal my defects, nor will I ever again judge them as harshly as once I did; for now I accept that they are no cause for shame. They have not the power to make me less valuable or deserving of love; they are but aspects of my human complexity.

I will give voice to my strengths and my frailties, for many may derive help and comfort from them. It is not for me to know who may most benefit; nor may I guess how my example may best serve them. The lesson I have now to learn is one of trust, and I trust that, in sharing myself with others, I give new hope and strength to them and myself alike.

I HAVE A VOICE THAT ENRICHES THE WORLD.

When the quicksand of misery came closest to sucking me down into oblivion, my tenacity in extricating myself was but a manifestation of the vitality and courage within me that will not be extinguished. Nevermore will my heart desert me. Henceforth I accept that my example provides a model of hope to others and even unto myself; for it is a reminder that the extremities we have overcome equip us to master all future challenges.

In truth I am furnished with resources in excess of what I may need in the days to come; I have but to draw on them and they will not fail me. I have but to lift up my voice and the power that lies within me multiplies.

I HAVE A VOICE THAT ENRICHES THE WORLD.

From this day on, I shall cherish my uniqueness, for thus may I help those around me to foster all that is most uniquely precious about themselves. And I shall cherish and protect my voice, that its beauty may be undimmed and its song an inspiration to my peers, my children, and myself.

I HAVE A VOICE THAT ENRICHES THE WORLD.

Week 11 Recorder

I have treated my thoughts, my feelings, and my words with due consideration. I have given voice to my wishes and needs and I have rejoiced in my place in the world.

Monday   Date

Number of times the Step was read:
Your score:
Total score:

Tuesday   Date

Number of times the Step was read:
Your score:
Total score:

Wednesday   Date

Number of times the Step was read:
Your score:
Total score:

THURSDAY   DATE

Number of times the Step was read:

Your score:

Total score:

FRIDAY   DATE

Number of times the Step was read:

Your score:

Total score:

Your end of week score:

QUOTATION

You feel most relevant to yourself this week:

_____
_____
_____
_____
_____
_____
_____
_____

Your achievements of the week:
_____
_____
_____
_____
_____
_____
_____
_____

Week 12 Recorder

I have treated my thoughts, my feelings, and my words with due consideration. I have given voice to my wishes and needs and I have rejoiced in my place in the world.

MONDAY   DATE

Number of times the Step was read: _____
Your score: _____
Total score: _____

TUESDAY   DATE

Number of times the Step was read: _____
Your score: _____
Total score: _____

WEDNESDAY   DATE

Number of times the Step was read: _____
Your score: _____
Total score: _____

THURSDAY   DATE

Number of times the Step was read:

Your score:

Total score:

FRIDAY   DATE

Number of times the Step was read:

Your score:

Total score:

Your end of week score:

QUOTATION

You feel most relevant to yourself this week:

_____
_____
_____
_____
_____
_____
_____
_____

Your achievements of the week:

_____
_____
_____
_____
_____
_____
_____
_____

Week 13 Recorder

I have treated my thoughts, my feelings, and my words with due consideration. I have given voice to my wishes and needs and I have rejoiced in my place in the world.

Monday   Date

Number of times the Step was read:
Your score:
Total score:

Tuesday   Date

Number of times the Step was read:
Your score:
Total score:

Wednesday   Date

Number of times the Step was read:
Your score:
Total score:

THURSDAY   DATE

Number of times the Step was read:

Your score:

Total score:

FRIDAY   DATE

Number of times the Step was read:

Your score:

Total score:

Your end of week score:

QUOTATION

You feel most relevant to yourself this week:

_____
_____
_____
_____
_____
_____
_____
_____

Your achievements of the week:
_____
_____
_____
_____
_____
_____
_____
_____

Week 14 Recorder

I have treated my thoughts, my feelings, and my words with due consideration. I have given voice to my wishes and needs and I have rejoiced in my place in the world.

MONDAY   DATE

Number of times the Step was read: _____
Your score: _____
Total score: _____

TUESDAY   DATE

Number of times the Step was read: _____
Your score: _____
Total score: _____

WEDNESDAY   DATE

Number of times the Step was read: _____
Your score: _____
Total score: _____

THURSDAY   DATE

Number of times the Step was read:

Your score:

Total score:

FRIDAY   DATE

Number of times the Step was read:

Your score:

Total score:

Your end of week score:

QUOTATION

You feel most relevant to yourself this week:

_____
_____
_____
_____
_____
_____
_____
_____

Your achievements of the week:

_____
_____
_____
_____
_____
_____
_____
_____

Week 15 Recorder

I have treated my thoughts, my feelings, and my words with due consideration. I have given voice to my wishes and needs and I have rejoiced in my place in the world.

MONDAY   DATE

Number of times the Step was read:
Your score:
Total score:

TUESDAY   DATE

Number of times the Step was read:
Your score:
Total score:

WEDNESDAY   DATE

Number of times the Step was read:
Your score:
Total score:

THURSDAY   DATE

Number of times the Step was read:

Your score:

Total score:

FRIDAY   DATE

Number of times the Step was read:

Your score:

Total score:

Your end of week score:

QUOTATION

You feel most relevant to yourself this week:

_____

_____

_____

_____

_____

_____

_____

Your achievements of the week:
_____
_____
_____
_____
_____
_____
_____
_____

Chapter 6

The Message Unheeded

Congratulations! You have completed another major leg of your journey. You've come a long way from when you started out and I'd like to honor the courage you have shown in venturing along this path away from the familiar harbor of the known. "Courage," Mark Twain observes, "is resistance to fear, mastery of fear, not absence of fear. Except a creature be part coward, it is not a compliment to say it is brave."

But does it feel like that to you? Maybe not. The thing is, you have been programmed to register weakness rather than strength, sameness rather than change. Habit dictates that you'll still see the same internal landscape even when its features have changed radically. So you're probably still picking up the things about yourself that you expect to see, the familiar sights on the landscape—the same old eyesores—and ignoring all the new building that's gone on.

If you just step past the edifice of self-doubt and turn the corner you'll see... what? A new development going up, in a new style of architecture that harmonizes buildings with their environment, that blends the beauty of nature with the best of timeless, man-made construction.

For too long now, you have been blind to yourself.

No doubt you could write a dissertation—or several—on your faults, limitations, defects, shortcomings, flaws, etc. But you miss the point: your frailties, such as they are, can never diminish your humanity, your value. At most, they diminish the credibility of the person, or persons, who have used them to undermine you. Your frailty simply serves to underscore your worth.

But it's hard to hold that belief for yourself. As E.E. Cummings notes, *"We do not believe in ourselves until someone reveals that deep inside us something is valuable, worth listening to, worthy of our trust, sacred to our touch. Once we believe in ourselves we can risk curiosity, wonder, spontaneous delight or any experience that reveals the human spirit."*

Over the next stage of the journey, you will learn to see your true image mirrored in the eyes and words of those around you, and you will start to understand something of the contribution you make to their lives.

I Am a Beacon of Light to Others

There was a woman who had grown up in a home where love was in short supply. She took many lessons from her upbringing.

She learned that she had no claim to her parents' love—that to meet with their approval, she needed to approach perfection as closely as she could. So she learned to be pretty and submissive, clean, tidy, and clever. She learned to think only about how she could please others and appease their demands. She learned especially that she would forfeit the little love she had if she was angry, opinionated, hurt or forthright. She learned always to walk on tiptoe for fear of stepping on anyone's feelings.

She learned never to have needs, because she saw what a heavy load she was for her parents to carry. She saw that the burden of their wisdom weighed heavily upon them and that they were too often disappointed by the shortcomings of their universe. She saw that she also disappointed them constantly.

She learned that there were no such things as minor infringements of the rules on which her parents' world revolved. She learned that the universe is black and white. And, in her heart of hearts, she always knew that she was black. Try as she may to be white, she knew she would be found out, that inevitably others one day would recognize the blackness in her heart. The fear was so great that she dared not even confess it.

She learned that her brothers and sisters were her rivals and that she could not turn for comfort to them, for they were all competing for the little share of love available and had none to spare themselves.

She learned that she was not loveable or special, not precious or worthy, but difficult, dull, unimportant and ordinary.

She learned that children are more burdensome than they are endearing.

She learned that, before she could hope to hear a word of love from anyone, she must acquiesce to their every demand.

She learned that relationships diminished more than they fulfilled her.

Yet for all that she grew to be a loving and much loved woman. She alone was blind to the love and regard in which she was held.

Her awakening was slow to begin, for she could not hear the inconceivable. Any word of criticism that was uttered roared in her head, yet she was deaf to expressions of her merit. She lived without the comfort of approval, because she lived without self-acceptance and her life was often intolerably hard.

At length she realized that she could not hear because she was not equipped to listen; she could not hear because she lacked the receptors required to pick up the frequency of approval.

Once it became clear to her that she had been excluded from the circle of acceptance by her lack of technology and not through any lack of personal worthiness, she set about making good that one deficiency. She set about installing the new receptors even before she attempted to divest herself of her old, obsolescent technology. Her new receptors she installed and programmed with but little faith, yet all the meticulousness of her dutiful nature.

The success of the operation would astound her. She had thought that change was available to others less blighted than herself, while she alone existed below the level of evolution and possibility. She found instead that she had installed technology and a program powerful enough to jam old signals and destroy her old receptors. And the messages she received delighted her more than she could ever have dared to imagine.

Step 5

I AM A BEACON OF LIGHT TO OTHERS.

No more will I substitute other people's feelings for my truth. In the past, people have voiced their negativity about their world and me, and I have wrongly deduced that their darkness was somehow my doing; that the child could be held responsible for the dissatisfactions of the adults. Now I see how their negativity dimmed their world and cast its shadow over me, their child. I see now that they could not let even the innocent light of childhood dispel their darkness and thus I concluded that I had no power to illuminate their world.

Instead I sought to dim my light, and perhaps I would even have extinguished it if I could have—for my yearning for acceptance was then so great that I would gladly have embraced their darkness. No longer will I let their darkness mask my light.

I AM A BEACON OF LIGHT TO OTHERS.

Nevermore will I be drawn towards the darkness. I am a creature of the light and henceforth will I seek out the light in which I may thrive. Now I see how my light has always attracted to me other fugitives from the darkness of despair and worthlessness and how they have benefited from my support even as I benefited from theirs.

I AM A BEACON OF LIGHT TO OTHERS.

In those years when I sought comfort and approval whence it would never be granted, I lost sight of myself. I saw only what I lacked—never what I had. I saw all of my defects, never any qualities. Nevermore will I prolong my search where it will not avail me. The loving support of friends made no impression on me, for I mistakenly believed that what I had not received, I could not deserve. My gratitude was unlimited for the light they cast over my existence, but never did I imagine that I too could enrich their lives.

From this day on I will trust that, as those I love bring light and joy into my life, so too do I bring the self-same gifts to theirs.

I AM A BEACON OF LIGHT TO OTHERS.

As I look at the love I bear my fellows, I realize how much my love is inspired by their uniqueness. I love them for the width of a smile, the readiness of their laugh, the openness of their gaze, the sadness in their eyes. I love them for their strength and their vulnerability, their gentleness and their hot temper, their humor and their seriousness, their serenity and their sadness, their hesitancy and their certainty. Each is uniquely precious to me not for how they hope to be or who they aspire to be. They are uniquely precious to me simply as they are.

So, too, is it with me. I too am loveable and loved simply as they see me. From this day on, I commit to learning to see and love myself as others love and see me.

I AM A BEACON OF LIGHT TO OTHERS.

As I love and value others with all their fears, their regrets, their self-doubts and frailties, so too will I love and value myself. For I see now that our frailty confers shape, depth, and luminosity; it does not diminish us. Only a lack of true love and care for the fragile essence of another can truly diminish the self.

My fortitude in acknowledging my past and working daily with my frailties allows my light to shine forth.

I AM A BEACON OF LIGHT TO OTHERS.

My sorrows and my joys, my anxieties and my certainties, my strengths and my weaknesses, my quirks and my conventionality comprise my unique humanity. Nothing that I have is more powerful than my humanity. Nothing that I can share is more valuable than my humanity. Knowledge, skills, status, and connections are mere accessories, tools whose value is determined by intention. It is not what I know but who I am that creates my unique, irreplaceable value.

I AM A BEACON OF LIGHT TO OTHERS.

From this day on, I accept that my light is bright enough to be seen, bright enough to serve as a landmark to others, bright enough to give faith and inspiration, even as others have given faith and inspiration to me.

I AM A BEACON OF LIGHT TO OTHERS.

From this day on, I undertake to cherish and nurture my unique humanity. Nevermore will I question my own worth, for what renders me valuable to others renders me valuable to myself in equal measure.

I AM A BEACON OF LIGHT TO OTHERS AND I WILL LET MY LIGHT SHINE FORTH.

Week 16 Recorder

I have endeavored to see myself as others see me. I have accepted that my light is bright enough to be seen and bright enough to serve as a landmark to others.

Monday   Date

Number of times the Step was read: _____
Your score: _____
Total score: _____

Tuesday   Date

Number of times the Step was read: _____
Your score: _____
Total score: _____

Wednesday   Date

Number of times the Step was read: _____
Your score: _____
Total score: _____

THURSDAY   DATE

Number of times the Step was read:

Your score:

Total score:

FRIDAY   DATE

Number of times the Step was read:

Your score:

Total score:

Your end of week score:

QUOTATION

You feel most relevant to yourself this week:

_____
_____
_____
_____
_____
_____
_____
_____

Your achievements of the week:

_____

_____

_____

_____

_____

_____

_____

Week 17 Recorder

I have endeavored to see myself as others see me. I have accepted that my light is bright enough to be seen and bright enough to serve as a landmark to others.

Monday   Date

Number of times the Step was read:
Your score:
Total score:

Tuesday   Date

Number of times the Step was read:
Your score:
Total score:

Wednesday   Date

Number of times the Step was read:
Your score:
Total score:

THURSDAY   DATE

Number of times the Step was read:

Your score:

Total score:

FRIDAY   DATE

Number of times the Step was read:

Your score:

Total score:

Your end of week score:

QUOTATION

You feel most relevant to yourself this week:

_____
_____
_____
_____
_____
_____
_____
_____

Your achievements of the week:
_____
_____
_____
_____
_____
_____
_____
_____

Week 18 Recorder

I have endeavored to see myself as others see me. I have accepted that my light is bright enough to be seen and bright enough to serve as a landmark to others.

Monday — DATE

Number of times the Step was read: _____

Your score: _____

Total score: _____

Tuesday — DATE

Number of times the Step was read: _____

Your score: _____

Total score: _____

Wednesday — DATE

Number of times the Step was read: _____

Your score: _____

Total score: _____

THURSDAY   DATE

Number of times the Step was read:

Your score:

Total score:

FRIDAY   DATE

Number of times the Step was read:

Your score:

Total score:

Your end of week score:

QUOTATION

You feel most relevant to yourself this week:

_____
_____
_____
_____
_____
_____
_____
_____

Your achievements of the week:

_____
_____
_____
_____
_____
_____
_____

Week 19 Recorder

I have endeavored to see myself as others see me. I have accepted that my light is bright enough to be seen and bright enough to serve as a landmark to others.

Monday   Date

Number of times the Step was read:

Your score:

Total score:

Tuesday   Date

Number of times the Step was read:

Your score:

Total score:

Wednesday   Date

Number of times the Step was read:

Your score:

Total score:

THURSDAY   DATE

Number of times the Step was read:

Your score:

Total score:

FRIDAY   DATE

Number of times the Step was read:

Your score:

Total score:

Your end of week score:

QUOTATION

You feel most relevant to yourself this week:

Your achievements of the week:
_____
_____
_____
_____
_____
_____
_____
_____

Week 20 Recorder

I have endeavored to see myself as others see me. I have accepted that my light is bright enough to be seen and bright enough to serve as a landmark to others.

Monday   DATE

Number of times the Step was read:
Your score:
Total score:

Tuesday   DATE

Number of times the Step was read:
Your score:
Total score:

Wednesday   DATE

Number of times the Step was read:
Your score:
Total score:

THURSDAY   DATE

Number of times the Step was read:

Your score:

Total score:

FRIDAY   DATE

Number of times the Step was read:

Your score:

Total score:

Your end of week score:

QUOTATION

You feel most relevant to yourself this week:

_____
_____
_____
_____
_____
_____
_____
_____

Your achievements of the week:
_____
_____
_____
_____
_____
_____
_____
_____

Chapter 7

Being the Difference

What's different?

Do you find that you're eager to take the next step along your journey? Are you curious to turn the pages of this book and discover what your next step will be? And what does that tell you about what's different about you?

Let's see. You could see that you feel more positive, that you're more optimistic—and leave it at that. If you do, your vision is still being colored by your old way of evaluating anything to do with you. So let's look at this together for a moment. In recent weeks, your status has changed dramatically: you see yourself as a survivor; you've become aware of your potential; you have reclaimed your voice; and you realize that you are an inspiration to others... and yourself. That's a pretty big shift.

Then there is what is going on in your life. You can't undergo such profound internal change without seeing it reflected in your life situations. People are starting to respond to you differently. Coincidence? I don't think so. More likely, other people have felt disposed to be warmer and more positive toward you because of the transformation in you.

The good things that you are starting to notice as isolated incidents are no such thing. What they are is part of a trend that you have set into motion. Let's be very clear about this: you have worked to create this trend; you have deserved it and you might as well get the most out of it.

Do you feel uncomfortable with that idea? You needn't. There is absolutely nothing wrong with claiming your full entitlement of joy, satisfaction, acknowledgement, etc. By doing so, you deprive no one. If you fail to do so, you will surely deprive yourself—and you will do so without benefiting anyone, save those who would feed on your weakness.

So acknowledge your achievement and take this opportunity to revise both your view of yourself and your expectations. You are the difference. Be the difference. Be prepared to challenge the old, low assessment of yourself that left you so hungry you were grateful to settle for crumbs. You don't have to settle for crumbs from anyone anymore; you have a feast laid at your own table. Now is the time to start savoring it. (Oh, and don't worry that if you eat too much now there won't be enough left for later. That feast is a creation of your own special brand of wizardry: it's self-replenishing.)

Back in the days when you had scant regard for yourself, you had scant regard for your time also. But that has changed. Your time is your life and it is to be prized, as you are. Your life is a precious vessel and from now on you will fill it only with those things that are of value to you.

From now on, it is for you to choose how you fill your life and to select only those things that strengthen and nurture you.

I Will Live My Best Life

A child was born into a family so dispossessed that the parents feared to give her anything, for fear of depriving themselves of what little there was. And so it was that they withheld from her… her very birth right.

It was the custom in that country for parents to fashion a mirror for their child so that the child could grow up seeing herself. That was what passed for self-knowledge in that land. Now, these parents were so hard-pressed by the struggle to survive that they thought they would save themselves another labor, so they found an old, abandoned mirror that, long before, had belonged to a relative. This mirror had been given to the relative by an elderly and malevolent grandmother—a witch—who had desired a meek and submissive child to serve her every whim. A magic spell ensured that the mirror would only ever return the image of a downcast, cowering child.

The parents knew something of the spell, but they felt that the power of the mirror could only serve their needs also, and so they polished the mirror as best they could and they gave it to their daughter. It would be, they thought, good enough for one whose birth entitled her to expect but little, and so they gave the matter no more thought as they labored to eke out their own meager existence.

The child grew to adulthood and she observed the customs of her land in all things, as was ever the way of the dispossessed. Her mirror hung from a nail where she could see herself in it and learn what manner of girl she was. In truth, what she saw saddened and humiliated her so that she could hardly bear to look. The image she glimpsed was that of a mere slip of a girl, a tiny creature cowering and hunched, with eyes downcast. From her mirror she learned, in the parlance of her land, that she was *"no better than she should be."*

She grew up a poor thing, a creature without aspirations—for what could a creature such as she aspire to? In time she married a fellow like her father and her life was not transformed; rather, it remained much as it had been before. For dowry she brought nothing but the mirror, which always reflected the same image of the tiny, hunched, cowering child. In truth she did not care to look into it much. When she did, she was mostly moved to gratitude. She would say to herself, *"I am fortunate indeed to have found a man like my husband willing to burden himself with such a sorry creature as I am. He is a good man, while I am but a millstone round his neck. I must never cease from doing all that I can to keep and please him."*

She spent her days in that endeavor, making sure that the best of what little they had always fell to her husband, and hoping for the occasional kind word, which came but rarely. Sometimes she would steel herself to look upon her image, and what she saw humbled her still further. *"Such a one as I am cannot expect kind words,"* she thought. *"It is enough if I escape blows, although even his blows I sometimes merit, due to my thoughtless words and careless actions."*

The woman's one concern was how to safeguard her place in her husband's home. She thought that if she could not bring him pleasure and win his heart, she could at least earn his tolerance by being as serviceable as she might. And so she drove herself ever harder. She resolved to work outside the home as well as in. She began to do the work of other women who had no need to tie their husband to them through humility and hard labor.

She became fascinated by these other women's lives, which she observed humbly, without thought of any needs or entitlement she herself might have. Nor did she entertain the dream of having a life such as theirs, for, poor creature that she was, she had long since ceased to dream her own dreams. The desire she harbored to be a perfect wife to her husband—and consequently blessed with happiness—had subsumed her very dreams.

Her life was hard and bitter, and grew increasingly so. Her husband reproached her, and if she turned to her mirror in the hope of some small comfort, always it reflected back to her the same sorry image of the cowering child. Yet now she found it harder every day to turn her eyes away from the image in the mirror—although, increasingly, the mirror drained her energies. It became harder and harder to drag herself through the myriad chores of her day. Try as she might, the image in the mirror remained unchanged and it was paralyzing her.

At length, when she had no strength left to stop herself from gazing listlessly at it, she resolved, at least when her husband when was not at home to see, to turn the mirror to the wall. It was a last attempt at preserving a sense of usefulness. The effort that it took her was disproportionate to the work involved. Before she could turn the mirror to the wall, she had first to combat the teachings of her family and her society. She had to challenge the customs of her country. Yet she did so driven by the hope of serving them better than before. Even one as downcast as she was needed some sense of usefulness to fuel her life.

She lifted the mirror off the nail and turned it over. Behind the silvered glass, she did not find rough wood as she had expected, but another mirrored surface in which she saw a female face, its lines etched deep by pain, but still a face that was strong, mobile, and beautiful. She hardly dared to gaze upon that face and hastily replaced the mirror on the wall. She noticed that the woman's arm moved as hers did, the face expressed the same surprise as hers, the mouth too moved when she spoke.

That day she did no work. She stood a long time before the mirror for she could not easily accept that the woman reflected in it might be her. She had always believed herself to be the tiny, hunched child with downcast eyes. The face reflected in the mirror gave her pause for thought. If she did not look as she had imagined, then she could not be the poor creature she had supposed. If she were not the poor creature she had supposed, then she would not live that wretched life. The vibrant woman she saw in the mirror was not made for a life of fear, humiliation, and servitude.

Now the woman began to see how greatly her past life had been blighted by the false image reflected in the enchanted mirror. She saw how greatly she had allowed herself to be limited by mistaken self-beliefs. She became aware that all the sadness, humiliations, and hurt of her past were past and need not encroach upon her future, and she resolved that she would evermore honor and cherish the woman she had discovered she truly was.

Step 6

I will live my best life.

In the past, I have let go of the reins of my life. I have allowed my dreams, my feelings, my vision, and my life to be overtaken by others, and I have lost my sense of self. I have lived as if I was a mere shadow of myself. I have projected into the world but a weak and pale reflection of the woman I truly am.

From this day on, I dare to dream my dreams. I dare to own my vision. I dare to hold center stage in my own life. I dare to choose the life that I want; and if I do not yet know how that life will look, still I dare to entertain a multitude of possibilities; I dare to explore all the different paths that are open to me.

I WILL LIVE MY BEST LIFE.

Nevermore will I reject my options even before I start to explore them. Nevermore will I say that I am too small and undeserving of the joys and riches that life can offer. My humanity is equal to that of every other person. My entitlement is as great as theirs. As I accept their worthiness without question, so now do I embrace my own.

I WILL LIVE MY BEST LIFE.

None can choose my life for me, but many may try. Others may seek to keep me as I once was, to serve their own self-interest. Some there are whose illusory sense of strength they have derived from my weakness. No longer will I allow others to feed on my flesh. Such people as these are likely to tell me how I put my security in danger. They will urge me to keep hold of the little that I had, for fear of being left with even less. In the past, I have bent to collect the straws that they scattered in their wake. I have clenched a few straws in my tightly closed fist so that I might hold something, and my hand has not been open to receive. From this day on, I open my hand.

I will live my best life.

No longer will I grasp at straws. No longer will I feed on crumbs. I will raise my eyes from the floor where they have long rested in my prostration and I will look on the richly laid table that stands in the vast hall wherein I live, for it is a table at which all have equal rights to sit. None may turn me away if I choose to sit at it. I will join the company at that table and I will feed and nurture myself as they do. There is space, sustenance, and companionship for all who will enjoy it.

I will live my best life.

My life from this day on may not always be without challenges, but I can choose my path and meet the difficulties that lie along it with confidence, knowing that my strength is equal to the task. The challenges I may face will be those that I have freely chosen—not burdens that have been imposed on me by others without due thought or care for my well-being.

I will live my best life.

Fear of failure cannot hold me back. I know now that the only failure is the paralysis of fear. The only failure is the refusal to take first one step, then another and another after that. The only humiliation is the impotence of immobility.

With each step, I dispel a little more of the fear that once bound me. Each step I now take towards a goal or dream is a small success. Each step brings me closer to my ultimate goal. It matters little whether or not I arrive at my initial destination; my momentum, my encounters along the way, and the vistas that open up before my eyes will all lead me towards the realization of my inmost dreams.

I WILL LIVE MY BEST LIFE.

From this day on, the strength and support that I need will be given to me. Mine is not a road that none has traveled before. My previous path of sorrow and despair also was much traveled but those who go along it are too weary and too downcast even to raise their eyes to notice the many others stumbling blindly down it. I will walk down my chosen path with joy and expectation. I will pool my resources with my fellow travelers and our resources will all be multiplied.

I WILL LIVE MY BEST LIFE.

On this day, I lift my eyes to encompass the beauty of the landscape and the multitude of my fellows. I will tread this path in joy and fellowship.

I CHOOSE TO LIVE MY BEST LIFE, AND MY EXAMPLE WILL EMPOWER OTHERS TO DO THE SAME.

Week 21 Recorder

I have dared to hold center stage in my own life and accepted my own worthiness. I have dared to dream my own dreams and own my own vision.

MONDAY   DATE

Number of times the Step was read: _____
Your score: _____
Total score: _____

TUESDAY   DATE

Number of times the Step was read: _____
Your score: _____
Total score: _____

WEDNESDAY   DATE

Number of times the Step was read: _____
Your score: _____
Total score: _____

THURSDAY　　　　　　　DATE

Number of times the Step was read:

Your score:

Total score:

FRIDAY　　　　　　　DATE

Number of times the Step was read:

Your score:

Total score:

Your end of week score:

QUOTATION

You feel most relevant to yourself this week:

_____
_____
_____
_____
_____
_____
_____

Your achievements of the week:

_____
_____
_____
_____
_____
_____
_____
_____

Week 22 Recorder

I have dared to hold center stage in my own life and accepted my own worthiness. I have dared to dream my own dreams and own my own vision.

Monday   DATE

Number of times the Step was read:
Your score:
Total score:

Tuesday   DATE

Number of times the Step was read:
Your score:
Total score:

Wednesday   DATE

Number of times the Step was read:
Your score:
Total score:

THURSDAY   DATE

Number of times the Step was read:

Your score:

Total score:

FRIDAY   DATE

Number of times the Step was read:

Your score:

Total score:

Your end of week score:

QUOTATION

You feel most relevant to yourself this week:

_____
_____
_____
_____
_____
_____
_____

Your achievements of the week:

_____
_____
_____
_____
_____
_____
_____
_____

Week 23 Recorder

I have dared to hold center stage in my own life and accepted my own worthiness. I have dared to dream my own dreams and own my own vision.

Monday   DATE

Number of times the Step was read: _____
Your score: _____
Total score: _____

Tuesday   DATE

Number of times the Step was read: _____
Your score: _____
Total score: _____

Wednesday   DATE

Number of times the Step was read: _____
Your score: _____
Total score: _____

THURSDAY   DATE

Number of times the Step was read:

Your score:

Total score:

FRIDAY   DATE

Number of times the Step was read:

Your score:

Total score:

Your end of week score:

QUOTATION

You feel most relevant to yourself this week:

_____
_____
_____
_____
_____
_____
_____
_____

Your achievements of the week:

_____
_____
_____
_____
_____
_____
_____
_____

Week 24 Recorder

I have dared to hold center stage in my own life and accepted my own worthiness. I have dared to dream my own dreams and own my own vision.

Monday   Date

Number of times the Step was read:
Your score:
Total score:

Tuesday   Date

Number of times the Step was read:
Your score:
Total score:

Wednesday   Date

Number of times the Step was read:
Your score:
Total score:

Thursday   Date

Number of times the Step was read: _____

Your score: _____

Total score: _____

Friday   Date

Number of times the Step was read: _____

Your score: _____

Total score: _____

Your end of week score:

Quotation

You feel most relevant to yourself this week:

_____
_____
_____
_____
_____
_____
_____

YOUR ACHIEVEMENTS OF THE WEEK:

_____
_____
_____
_____
_____
_____
_____
_____

Week 25 Recorder

I have dared to hold center stage in my own life and accepted my own worthiness. I have dared to dream my own dreams and own my own vision.

Monday   DATE

Number of times the Step was read: _____
Your score: _____
Total score: _____

Tuesday   DATE

Number of times the Step was read: _____
Your score: _____
Total score: _____

Wednesday   DATE

Number of times the Step was read: _____
Your score: _____
Total score: _____

THURSDAY   DATE

Number of times the Step was read:

Your score:

Total score:

FRIDAY   DATE

Number of times the Step was read:

Your score:

Total score:

Your end of week score:

QUOTATION

You feel most relevant to yourself this week:

_____
_____
_____
_____
_____
_____
_____
_____

YOUR ACHIEVEMENTS OF THE WEEK:

_____
_____
_____
_____
_____
_____
_____
_____

Chapter 8

Embrace the Miraculous

Have you noticed how much happiness has come into your life over the time that we've been working together?

You didn't set out to look for it; you didn't sit back and hope it would come to you—and yet there is a lot more joy in your life. Does that surprise you? Maybe it doesn't look like you thought happiness would. Helen Keller writes, *"When one door of happiness closes, another opens; but often we look so long at the closed door that we do not see the one which has been opened."* Especially if the door on which your eyes are fixed is the grand entrance to the palace of relationship bliss.

And what if the door that has opened is simply the modest door to a modest building? It's easy, then, to overlook the true nature of the feeling it evokes in you. The modest, even humble, building may not be what you had in mind, but for all you know it could be a dwelling of simple beauty. Equally, it could be the gatehouse to a magnificent estate with woods, landscaped gardens, a castle... It may not be your exclusive enclave but part of the common heritage. Does the fact that it is not exclusively yours make it any less beautiful and precious, or is it a further reason to give thanks?

"Happiness is itself a kind of gratitude," according to Joseph Wood Krutch, and gratitude is itself a choice. For Albert Einstein, "There are only two ways to live your life. One is as though nothing is a miracle. The other is as though everything is a miracle." You've tested the first way and experienced its effect on your life and your spirit. The road to self-recovery is a journey along the other way.

You are free, now, to embrace the miracle; you can choose gratitude.

On This Day I Choose Happiness

There was a woman who grew up in a country where the sun mostly shone. She delighted in its warmth; she reveled in its golden rays. She bore it a deep, abiding love. It filled her life with light and color.

A time came when the woman moved to another country, away from her beloved Mediterranean shores. She moved to a gray, Northern land where she sought to create a new life for herself. But it was a country where the rain fell long and hard for days and weeks at a time. The woman suffered deeply. She had not prepared herself for rain. She had counted on a life into which little rain would ever fall and she knew not how she could survive the bad weather. She resolved to hide away and wait for the sun to return, for then she would surely be happy. So she took refuge in a room. She would put her life on hold until the sun came out.

The woman grew old and disconsolate as she gazed out through her window and waited. But the sun could not change its course to satisfy her longing. So powerful was her longing that most of her life had gone by before she understood this. Then she saw that she had focused solely on the fulfillment of that one thing she most yearned for, and in doing so she had abdicated her share of happiness…

Step 7

On this day I choose happiness.

In the past I have known much pain and sorrow. Unhappiness and dissatisfaction have been my constant companions. My past I cannot change. My present circumstances are still informed by past emotions and I cannot transform them overnight. But from this moment on, I choose my feelings.

On this day I choose happiness.

As I choose my feelings, so do I embrace my power to transform my external circumstances. No more will feelings of sorrow and despair overwhelm me. No more will my sense of self be at the mercy of an implied criticism, a cruel word, a negative judgment. Henceforth I will cast off the harsh self-judgments that too long have oppressed me.

For too long have I experienced how the power of negative thought works to create an injurious reality. From today I believe in my faith and conviction that life has much joy to offer me. I have the power to attract into my life the good that I desire. I know that I am deserving of joy, and henceforth I will welcome it as my portion of life's riches.

On this day I choose happiness.

I am my own support. No longer will I hang on every word spoken to me in my search for the crumbs of comfort that never suffice to sate my hunger. No longer will I beseech others for the expressions of care and consideration that until today I had never bestowed upon myself. No longer will I imitate the cruelty of those who have chosen to deny me loving-kindness, by withholding it from myself also.

From this day on, I will nurture myself with the same love and care as I nurture others. I will nourish my sense of self with gentle words, kind thoughts, and a constant diet of joys both great and small.

On this day I choose happiness.

No more will I live in a world where it falls to me to protect the fragile and exacting feelings of those around me. No more will I sacrifice myself, making do even without the sustenance I need to safeguard my well-being, for fear of causing hurt or slight to others. No more will I tell myself that my feelings are inconsequential, even as I watch over the fragile feelings of others as jealously as if they were made of the finest porcelain.

I see now the confusion that reigned in my mind over needs and feelings: those around me, I learned, had feelings that were to be respected at all costs, whereas my needs, were I to mention them, would place an intolerable burden on others.

In my naivety, I let myself be duped into believing that others' demands were feelings, always to be put before my own. In my ignorance, I believed that I alone had no claim to care, consideration, or contentment.

No longer will I allow others' demands to eclipse my legitimate needs. No longer will I force my spirit to struggle for survival in the barren soil of a joyless existence.

On this day I choose happiness.

My children's needs are paramount and these will I gladly meet. As my children grow, so will I teach them to nurture themselves, and this I believe I can best do by offering them my example of self-consideration to emulate. Henceforth I respect and embrace my own needs and these are now sacrosanct to me, in word and deed. Paramount among them, from this moment on, will be my need to experience the full measure of joy that each day contains.

On this day I choose happiness.

In the past my unvoiced needs rose up to overwhelm me. They clamored to be met, yet I denied them daily until the silt of despair came close to choking life itself out of me.

Now I know that there is no shame in having needs. I see that I honor myself when I acknowledge my needs with honesty; when I gently ask that others take heed of them also; when I request to meet with the same respectful consideration that I show to others. This is but part of my entitlement by virtue of my humanity, and from this moment on I shall claim it.

As I honor my needs, so do I throw off the negative feelings that previously held me in thrall. As I open myself up to my true nature, as I own my humanity, even with its share of frailty, so do I open myself up to life's joys.

On this day I choose happiness.

There are people to whom much has been given who yet defer their happiness to a future in which all the circumstances of their life will be perfect. They are seekers after an absolute. They defer joy until they can fit into place every last piece of their vision. Always their attention is drawn to the pieces that they lack. Happiness is always outside and just beyond their reach.

No more will I pursue a mirage of happiness. No more will I be numbered among the seekers after a beautiful tomorrow whose quest is doomed to disappointment.

I will not be as they are. I will not waste the precious days in urgent pursuit of an elusive dream.

On this day I choose happiness.

From today I espouse a different vision of happiness. I now believe that routing critical thoughts and negative emotions is enough to create a climate in which happiness can flourish, and this I shall do.

Each day, and even several times in the day, I shall rehearse the reasons I have to celebrate. I will rejoice in my children, my friends, my health, a ray of sunshine, music, shared laughter, the beauty of a flower, the poetry of the moment. Henceforth I will set store by loving words, acts of kindness, chance good fortune. I will own all the good that I do and I will celebrate all the good that is done to me and to those whom I love in the course of each day. All the small gifts in my day that I once carelessly overlooked I now celebrate, for they will multiply my joy and they attract ever more blessings into my life.

On this day I choose happiness.

And the celebration of present joys, driving all thoughts of past hardships from my mind, will make me whole.

Week 26 Recorder

I nurtured myself with the same love and care as I nurtured others and I nourished myself with gentle words, kind thoughts, and a diet of joys, both great and small.

Monday   DATE

Number of times the Step was read: _____
Your score: _____
Total score: _____

Tuesday   DATE

Number of times the Step was read: _____
Your score: _____
Total score: _____

Wednesday   DATE

Number of times the Step was read: _____
Your score: _____
Total score: _____

THURSDAY   DATE

Number of times the Step was read:

Your score:

Total score:

FRIDAY   DATE

Number of times the Step was read:

Your score:

Total score:

Your end of week score:

QUOTATION

You feel most relevant to yourself this week:

_____
_____
_____
_____
_____
_____
_____
_____

Your achievements of the week:
_____
_____
_____
_____
_____
_____
_____
_____

Week 27 Recorder

I nurtured myself with the same love and care as I nurtured others and I nourished myself with gentle words, kind thoughts, and a diet of joys, both great and small.

Monday   Date

Number of times the Step was read:
Your score: _____
Total score: _____
_____

Tuesday   Date

Number of times the Step was read:
Your score: _____
Total score: _____
_____

Wednesday   Date

Number of times the Step was read:
Your score: _____
Total score: _____
_____

THURSDAY　　　　　　　　　DATE

Number of times the Step was read:

Your score:

Total score:

FRIDAY　　　　　　　　　　DATE

Number of times the Step was read:

Your score:

Total score:

Your end of week score:

QUOTATION

You feel most relevant to yourself this week:

_____
_____
_____
_____
_____
_____
_____

Your achievements of the week:
_____
_____
_____
_____
_____
_____
_____
_____

Week 28 Recorder

I nurtured myself with the same love and care as I nurtured others and I nourished myself with gentle words, kind thoughts, and a diet of joys, both great and small.

MONDAY   DATE

Number of times the Step was read: _____

Your score: _____

Total score: _____

TUESDAY   DATE

Number of times the Step was read: _____

Your score: _____

Total score: _____

WEDNESDAY   DATE

Number of times the Step was read: _____

Your score: _____

Total score: _____

THURSDAY   DATE

Number of times the Step was read:

Your score:

Total score:

FRIDAY   DATE

Number of times the Step was read:

Your score:

Total score:

Your end of week score:

QUOTATION

You feel most relevant to yourself this week:

_____
_____
_____
_____
_____
_____
_____
_____

Your achievements of the week:

_____
_____
_____
_____
_____
_____
_____
_____

Week 29 Recorder

I nurtured myself with the same love and care as I nurtured others and I nourished myself with gentle words, kind thoughts, and a diet of joys, both great and small.

MONDAY   DATE

Number of times the Step was read:
Your score: _____
Total score: _____

TUESDAY   DATE

Number of times the Step was read:
Your score: _____
Total score: _____

WEDNESDAY   DATE

Number of times the Step was read:
Your score: _____
Total score: _____

THURSDAY   DATE

Number of times the Step was read:

Your score:

Total score:

FRIDAY   DATE

Number of times the Step was read:

Your score:

Total score:

Your end of week score:

QUOTATION

You feel most relevant to yourself this week:

_____
_____
_____
_____
_____
_____
_____

Your achievements of the week:

_____
_____
_____
_____
_____
_____
_____
_____

Week 30 Recorder

I nurtured myself with the same love and care as I nurtured others and I nourished myself with gentle words, kind thoughts, and a diet of joys, both great and small.

Monday   DATE

Number of times the Step was read: _____
Your score: _____
Total score: _____

Tuesday   DATE

Number of times the Step was read: _____
Your score: _____
Total score: _____

Wednesday   DATE

Number of times the Step was read: _____
Your score: _____
Total score: _____

THURSDAY   DATE

Number of times the Step was read:

Your score:

Total score:

FRIDAY   DATE

Number of times the Step was read:

Your score:

Total score:

Your end of week score:

QUOTATION

You feel most relevant to yourself this week:

_____
_____
_____
_____
_____
_____
_____

Your achievements of the week:

_____
_____
_____
_____
_____
_____
_____
_____

Chapter 9

Expect Abundance

Are you still selling yourself short, even after all this time?

Certainly your self-worth has improved exponentially. You now begin to realize what a uniquely precious and gifted person you are—but what about your expectations?

What does your vision of your future look like? Do your expectations match your new self-image or are they still inspired by a conviction of scarcity? Do you still assume that, despite the transformation you are undergoing, you can look forward to a life of struggle because you have struggled in the past? Isn't it time to let go of the struggle mindset?

Pascal observed, *"Our achievements of today are but the sum total of our thoughts of yesterday. You are today where the thoughts of yesterday have brought you and you will be tomorrow where the thoughts of today take you."* So why not let them take you where you desire to be, rather than where you fear to be?

You wouldn't seriously expect to be able to travel with an outdated airline ticket, especially when it's within your power to issue yourself with a new, valid one at any time.

Your expectations are your ticket on your journey of self-recovery. Why not issue yourself with a ticket for the destination of your dreams? You only have to revise your expectations. If you are not sure how to, let Eileen Caddy instruct you: *"Expect your every need to be met, expect the answer to every problem, expect abundance on every level, expect to grow spiritually."*

I Live in a World of Love and Abundance

A child was born who could spin chaff into gold. It was discovered like this: as a tiny child, she once sat on the floor of her father's barn, her toy spindle in her little hand, playing quietly while her parents worked. And as she played, she produced a fine gold thread.

When her father saw what she had done, he was mightily afraid. He had worked all his life to produce the little that he had and now a tiny child had called it into question. He took the toy spindle from her and told his wife that the child spent too much time alone. She needed company; she needed younger brothers and sisters she could play with and look after.

In due course the couple had many sons and their daughter was a little mother to them. She loved and cared for them. She did their bidding. She saw that it was her lot in life to be a helpmate. She knew that, at some point, a young man would come, a poor farmer like her father, to ask for her hand. She would go and share his life, as she had done her parents'.

In time a young man duly came. He saw that the girl was fair. He saw that the parents were fecund. He talked at length with the parents and learned that they had brought the girl up to be dutiful, hard-working, and selfless. He thought she would suit him very well.

So the young man married the girl and set her to be dutiful, hard-working, and selfless in his home, in a village many miles from where her parents lived. Once there, using all the blandishments that newlyweds use, he acquainted her with her new life and her new responsibilities.

Now, from her infancy, the father had nevermore let the girl touch a spindle. But he had not spoken of this to the young man. Years had passed and he dared to hope his daughter had forgotten what had happened; he dared to hope that she had lost the gift of her earliest years.

The girl settled into her new life and accepted her husband and master gladly. The young man congratulated himself on his choice, and through the first summer months, their lives passed uneventfully. The day came, however, when the girl sat at her spindle. At first she spun only in the normal way and all went well. But late one evening when she was all but dozing over her wheel, she thought, or dreamed, that she might help her young husband by creating something of value from the chaff also. She spun a few handfuls, hardly knowing what she did, and it turned to gold.

But the husband was not as the father. When he saw what she had done, he stayed very quiet. He did not berate her. He did not snatch the spindle from her hand. But nor did he make exclamations and praise her. He merely said that she looked tired and urged her to rest, so as to be strong and fit for the tasks of the morrow.

Alone with the gold thread, the husband sat and thought. He told himself he wished at all costs to avoid upheaval in the relationship with his young wife, for she served him well and pleased him also. He told himself that nothing need change in their life together; it could continue still as it had been before. But he was not as her father; he would not tell her never again to spin chaff into gold. Instead, he said to himself, *"On this day my young wife has become yet more precious to me. So precious, in fact, that my fear of losing her grows very great, greater than I would wish her to know. But how can I secure her and, with her, how am I to secure also all the good that she bestows on me?"*

After much thought, he resolved to treat her spinning as though it were without value. He would make her understand that it revealed a grave flaw in her character. A good wife, he said, proved her virtue by staying within the usual limits in all things; she did neither more nor less than her husband required; a good wife obeyed her master's needs and wishes unquestioningly, and never interpreted or changed them. Living as they did on a farm at the edge of a small village, his wife had limited occasion to speak with other womenfolk.

But from that moment on, the husband determined that he was best served by keeping his wife utterly apart from all those who dwelled beyond his home.

Accordingly, he settled upon a plan: he would continually reprove his wife's shortcomings and criticize the fruits of her labors, and he would keep from her all evidence of his increase in wealth; rather, he would reduce the meager comforts of their home and tell her repeatedly that the little they had was constantly being eaten away.

He and he alone would be the messenger carrying all information from the outside world to her, and every bulletin would testify to their increasing hardship and her defects of character and conduct—flaws so gross that village society had registered them even at such remove, simply by observing how her husband and her home had declined in fortune under her stewardship. The wife was mortified by the reports he bore, but she was as devoted as she was dutiful. She strove ever harder to bring comfort into the home and win the good opinion of her husband and of that world in which she no longer wished to show her face.

Her efforts were fruitless and the wife grew dumb with shame. Her loathing of herself became so complete that she would beg repeatedly for just one word of kindness from her husband. She toiled night and day without meeting with his approval and without increase in her circumstances. She cooked and cleaned, she cared for her home and the animals, and spun without repose and without thought for herself. Ever harder did she work herself while her husband's coffers grew full, and ever more harshly did he blame her for her laziness and the grinding poverty to which she had reduced him.

So, even as the husband thrived in secret, the wife was overwhelmed by the evidence that she was burdensome and valueless. She despaired almost unto death. Despair prostrated her until she had no strength left to fight, until she accepted without demur that she was as vile, worthless, and selfish as her husband painted her.

Only when she accepted that she was a worm and a parasite feeding on her husband did she finally accept her humanity also. Only then did she truly accept that she also had a right to live, however base she might be. When she learned acceptance, she ceased to fear the reproaches with which her husband had laid her low. She ceased being cowed by shame.

She ceased being terrified by the specter of scarcity. Slowly she found a voice that grew ever clearer, purer, stronger, louder as she exercised it daily, until it drowned out her husband's reproaches, until it deafened him and exposed his cruelty and deceit, his petty machinations.

The woman lifted up her voice and its clear timbre shattered the edifice of lies and scarcity in which her husband had incarcerated her, and the beauty of that voice, which was a true reflection of the woman's soul, fashioned a new world around her of love, admiration, and plenty.

Step 8

I LIVE IN A WORLD OF LOVE AND ABUNDANCE.

In the past I have lived in the shadow of fear and fear has blinkered me. My fear has left me blind to everything but scarcity. Fear has caused me to see only scarcity in my past and it has led me to believe that the present and the future hold no more for me than scarcity. I have seen that others enjoy sufficiency, yet I have believed that I alone was excluded from that world. From this day on, I share the same air, the same sky, the same climate, the same plenty as do they.

I LIVE IN A WORLD OF LOVE AND ABUNDANCE.

I was misled into mistaking fear for reality. I learned that fear is wisdom. I was educated to confuse fear with certainty. I was taught that I have but little and that that meager portion could be snatched away from me at any time.

In the past I have embraced false beliefs. I have been blind to the evidence of my own eyes. Yet all around me there is abundance for those who truly desire it and who base their actions on the firm conviction that they are worthy of it.

No more will I be the hungry child staring in at the window of those whose home is blessed with comfort, warmth, love, and plenitude. No more will I treat myself as but a beggar at the gate.

From this day on, I know that I am deserving of ease and plenty.

I LIVE IN A WORLD OF LOVE AND ABUNDANCE.

No past scarcity can rob me of future abundance. It is for me to choose how I view my world. The difficulties of what has gone before do not condition my future. I now choose to create my future and that future will not be as my past was. I put behind me the dark world of destitution and fear. I step out of deprivation and into plenty. Instead of fear I choose trust in a good outcome; in place of isolation I choose fellowship; instead of despair I choose faith; instead of hardship I choose well-being, instead of misery I choose joy.

I LIVE IN A WORLD OF LOVE AND ABUNDANCE.

I know now that I am deserving of life's greatest good. There is none too small and worthless to have any claim on love and abundance. My humanity is my entitlement and it is absolute. It is equal to that of every other human being. I do not ask others to confer joy and plenty on me. That is something that I can do for myself and I will. But none may deny me what is rightfully mine. From this day on, no man or woman can impose their choices on me. I and I alone create my vision of the world and the place I hold in it.

I LIVE IN A WORLD OF LOVE AND ABUNDANCE.

From now on I take responsibility for opening my heart and mind to allow love and abundance into my life. I cannot remedy another person's scarcity. If those around me will focus on what they lack, I cannot change that. I am not responsible for their joy or their misery. I am powerless to change their thoughts. No longer will I strive fruitlessly to help them. No longer will I try to supplement their deficiencies by my exuberance. From this day on, I will nurture myself, knowing that as I extend care and love to myself, so will it be given to me. I renounce futility. The seeds of my abundance are too precious to be cast on arid ground. I plant them where they will prosper and multiply.

I LIVE IN A WORLD OF LOVE AND ABUNDANCE.

In the past I have lavished my treasures on others without thought for myself or for the morrow, and others have taken from me all that I had. I had thought that what had been given to me was devoid of worth except when it was bestowed on others. Now I see that what I do not cherish will never be cherished, even by those who benefit from it. Henceforth I will cherish the gifts that are mine and those gifts will be multiplied beyond anything my mind can presently conceive.

I LIVE IN A WORLD OF LOVE AND ABUNDANCE.

Abundance is new to me and I may not always recognize the forms it takes. There may be times when my vision fails me and all around me I see the specters of past scarcity. Even then will I trust that to me will be given what I need to keep alive not just my body, but my dreams and my soul also. My faith is like a flame that burns deep within me; it may flicker at times, it may wane, but it will not be extinguished, for I have replaced the old stifling belief in scarcity with the oxygen of my new faith.

I LIVE IN A WORLD OF LOVE AND ABUNDANCE.

From this day on, I am aware of all the love that surrounds me. No more will I fix my quest for love on just one person to the exclusion of all others. No more will I undervalue the love of my family and my friends. No more will I be blind to the precious love of my children. No more will I let the kindnesses and acts of love of acquaintances and even strangers pass unnoticed. No act of love is so small that I may not rejoice at it.

From this day on, I will meet each word and act of care and kindness with love and acknowledgement.

I LIVE IN A WORLD OF LOVE AND ABUNDANCE AND I UNDERTAKE TO GIVE AND RECEIVE THESE BLESSINGS TO THE FULLEST.

Week 31 Recorder

I have opened my heart and my mind to allow love and abundance into my life. I have nurtured myself, knowing that as I extend care and love to myself, so will it be given to me.

Monday   Date

Number of times the Step was read:

Your score:

Total score:

Tuesday   Date

Number of times the Step was read:

Your score:

Total score:

Wednesday   Date

Number of times the Step was read:

Your score:

Total score:

THURSDAY   DATE

Number of times the Step was read:

Your score:

Total score:

FRIDAY   DATE

Number of times the Step was read:

Your score:

Total score:

Your end of week score:

QUOTATION

You feel most relevant to yourself this week:

_____

_____

_____

_____

_____

_____

_____

Your achievements of the week:

_____
_____
_____
_____
_____
_____
_____
_____
_____

Week 32 Recorder

I have opened my heart and my mind to allow love and abundance into my life. I have nurtured myself, knowing that as I extend care and love to myself, so will it be given to me.

Monday   DATE

Number of times the Step was read: _____

Your score: _____

Total score: _____

Tuesday   DATE

Number of times the Step was read: _____

Your score: _____

Total score: _____

Wednesday   DATE

Number of times the Step was read: _____

Your score: _____

Total score: _____

Thursday   Date

Number of times the Step was read:

Your score:

Total score:

Friday   Date

Number of times the Step was read:

Your score:

Total score:

Your end of week score:

Quotation

You feel most relevant to yourself this week:

_____
_____
_____
_____
_____
_____
_____

Your achievements of the week:

_____
_____
_____
_____
_____
_____
_____
_____

Week 33 Recorder

I have opened my heart and my mind to allow love and abundance into my life. I have nurtured myself, knowing that as I extend care and love to myself, so will it be given to me.

Monday   DATE

Number of times the Step was read:
Your score:
Total score:

Tuesday   DATE

Number of times the Step was read:
Your score:
Total score:

Wednesday   DATE

Number of times the Step was read:
Your score:
Total score:

Thursday   Date

Number of times the Step was read:

Your score:

Total score:

Friday   Date

Number of times the Step was read:

Your score:

Total score:

Your end of week score:

Quotation

You feel most relevant to yourself this week:

_____

_____

_____

_____

_____

_____

_____

Your achievements of the week:

_____
_____
_____
_____
_____
_____
_____
_____

Week 34 Recorder

I have opened my heart and my mind to allow love and abundance into my life. I have nurtured myself, knowing that as I extend care and love to myself, so will it be given to me.

MONDAY   DATE

Number of times the Step was read:

Your score:

Total score:

TUESDAY   DATE

Number of times the Step was read:

Your score:

Total score:

WEDNESDAY   DATE

Number of times the Step was read:

Your score:

Total score:

## THURSDAY					DATE

Number of times the Step was read:

Your score:

Total score:

## FRIDAY					DATE

Number of times the Step was read:

Your score:

Total score:

Your end of week score:

QUOTATION

You feel most relevant to yourself this week:

_____
_____
_____
_____
_____
_____
_____

_____

Your achievements of the week:

_____
_____
_____
_____
_____
_____
_____
_____

Week 35 Recorder

I have opened my heart and my mind to allow love and abundance into my life. I have nurtured myself, knowing that as I extend care and love to myself, so will it be given to me.

Monday   DATE

Number of times the Step was read:

Your score: _____

Total score: _____

Tuesday   DATE

Number of times the Step was read:

Your score: _____

Total score: _____

Wednesday   DATE

Number of times the Step was read:

Your score: _____

Total score: _____

THURSDAY   DATE

Number of times the Step was read:

Your score:

Total score:

FRIDAY   DATE

Number of times the Step was read:

Your score:

Total score:

Your end of week score:

QUOTATION

You feel most relevant to yourself this week:

_____
_____
_____
_____
_____
_____
_____

Your achievements of the week:

_____
_____
_____
_____
_____
_____
_____
_____

Chapter 10

You Are the Armorer

Do you ever stop to think about how dynamic you are?

Perhaps the time has come to do just that or, more to the point, to begin to register your dynamism. Maybe you have started to notice the positive effect you have on the people around you. But what about your children? I wonder if you have truly recognized the impact you have on them—and especially the impact you have for good.

"You are the bows," writes Khalil Gibran, *"from which your children as living arrows are sent forth."*

What a telling image that is, and how different from the way you have habitually viewed your role. You could hardly fail to undervalue your parenting when you undervalued yourself, but now you are in a position to see that you are as precious a gift to your children as they are to you.

Your children have given you many things in return for the love, care, and time that you have invested in them. It may be that you still feel some regret for the things you could not give them at a stage in your life when you were so harried that you had little to give to another and still less for your own sustenance. Your regret, now, serves neither them nor you.

You have come so far. You are free now to shed these old regrets, to slough off the old stunted persona that no longer fits you. The moment has come to own the greatest gifts that you have to offer your children.

Know that the blessings that you now give them are supremely valuable. Your self-recovery teaches them to armor themselves against cruelty and contempt, and safeguards them from present and future harm. You have provided them with an example and become a role model for them, inspiring them to grow freely and reach their full potential with love, courage, and faith in a better future. Your actions have broken the mold that could have oppressed them throughout all their days and oppressed their children also after them.

"Thousands of candles can be lighted from a single candle" (Buddha).

What you have achieved with courage and struggle is your gift to posterity also.

My Children Will Wear Golden Armor

A child was born into a family where there had been much disharmony, yet she was a wanted child. The father especially believed he must have a child to make his life complete. The mother, oppressed by the burden of her husband's wrath, his constant disapproval, was greatly concerned. Many a time had her husband told her she was not woman enough to be a wife to him, yet she had clung to him in love and shame and paroxysms of despair. Now she was greatly frightened that she would not prove woman enough to be a mother to her child, as he so often hinted.

The child was born and she brought a love and joy previously unimaginable to the mother's heart, and the mother made a solemn vow that the daughter's life would be far, far more blessed than her own.

"It is too late for me," she reasoned. *"My bed is made and I must lie in it. None but my husband could bear with such a one as me. I am but a worm; without his love I am nothing. But I shall ensure that my daughter has a far better life than ever I did."*

So the woman brought the child up as best she could, and surrounded her with as much love and care as she was able. From her earliest years, the child delighted all who met her; she brought joy and light everywhere she went. She and her mother bore each other a deep and tender love that was remarked upon by all, and moved all, save one. That one was her father.

As the father watched the child grow, he became evermore deeply jealous of the love between his wife and daughter. That love, he felt, both slighted and excluded him, for if he was not the apple of his daughter's eye, he was nothing. He began to rage against his daughter in his heart and he tried in every way he could to sow discord between his wife and child.

Sometimes he succeeded in sowing discord and then he showered his child with love and praise. More commonly he failed, and then, increasingly, he would turn his wrath on her, while trying to poison the mother's mind. He would show his child a loving face in front of her mother, but when he was alone with his daughter he would talk at length of all the cruel deaths that befell little children. He would fill her head with hardship and suffering and would even threaten to beat her, telling her that if she tried to detail his cruelty, she would not be able to make her mother believe a word of it.

And so it was, for when he was being most cruel to the child, he would show a brief affection for the mother. She, poor creature, was as gullible as he was duplicitous. Moreover, she was a starving woman who gladly gathered up whatever crumbs of affection he threw her way. Often he profited from her gratitude to denounce their child's shortcomings. He would say, *"The child comes between us. She is too needy, too demanding. She lacks respect for her father. She is two-faced. You are easily deceived, but I see her as she really is. Your love will destroy her."*

To the child he would say, *"You cannot know how much I have longed for a son. There is so much that I could share with my son. You are your mother's child. A son would respect me and look up to me."* He described the tender love he would have shown a son so that his daughter suffered torments; for she believed that if he showed her fury and not love, the fault was hers. She grew up believing that even tiny children can fail their parents most grievously.

Theirs was a joyless home. The father declared himself thwarted in his capacity for love and pleasure by the infinite shortcomings of his wife and daughter, and they felt as though all they touched turned to dust and ashes.

The child became evermore downcast. Her father's cruelty ate away at her very soul so that the light that shone from her being dwindled and waned. She had learned to bow her head before cruelty, and cruelty increasingly found her. The marks of her upbringing were written on her brow and many who delighted in cruelty were drawn toward her.

Still, the mother so lacked faith in herself that she could not uphold the good of the child. The father alone had clarity, vision, certainty, faith in himself and in his pronouncements.

It came about that his carelessness undid him. A time came when he no longer felt obliged to veil his contempt, when he ceased proffering the last crumbs of affection and concern. Then the wife became the merest shadow of herself and she despised herself even as much as her husband despised her.

She resolved that she must reclaim her human dignity, her soul, or endure a living death of shame, misery, and loneliness. She knew that she could do so only by overthrowing his influence, by driving him from her world.

It took every vestige of her courage to do so. She had believed that she needed him to fill the void of her world. Now she found that, in the unbounded space left by his departure, she had room to grow.

She grew. Slowly and fearfully at first, and then faster and more spontaneously. She grew into the woman she truly was, a woman she could love, respect, and trust. As she grew, so too did her child.

Cruel people still sought to hurt the child, but now the mother stood beside her. The mother vowed that nevermore would her child be exposed to cruelty, and so, out of her love and regret, she forged a suit of golden armor. The mother taught the child to don the golden armor so that barbs and blows bounced off it without harming her, and the child learned to be safe. She learned to love and grow. She learned to trust that she was strong and good enough. She learned also that cruel people had lost their power over her. She looked out from under her golden helmet and saw all the frailty of the cruel. No longer could they touch her, and she saw them for what they were.

She had become free to walk her own path, dream her own dreams, and create her own world. The mother watched her venture forth in her golden armor and rejoiced. She had given her child the greatest gift it was hers to give.

Step 9

My children will wear golden armor.

It has always been my wish for my children to have a golden future, and I cherished that dream so dearly that I could not see how dark their present had become.

I sought to protect my children, even when I was not able to protect my own physical, emotional, and spiritual well-being. I could not know then that what I was not able to do for myself, I could not do for any other.

In the days when my torment was so great, I saw not the extent of my children's anguish. Nor did I wish to see it, for it comforted me to believe that my torment remained concealed from them. My one consolation was my hope that my children's innocence would be spared, that they would be unscathed by the brutality and cruelty of their home.

My Children Will Wear Golden Armor.

Nevermore will I offer nothing more solid than a wish to safeguard their innocence. Nevermore will I think that I am serving their interest by concealing my pain and thus condoning the cruelty of another.

Nevermore will I undermine them by offering them an example of fear and powerlessness.

Nevermore will I teach them, by my example, to meet contempt with acceptance.

My Children Will Wear Golden Armor.

I cannot rewrite my children's past, but together we can rewrite their future. Despite all that they have witnessed in the past, they can inhabit a world of courage and joy, for that is their birthright. From out of the depths of my abasement, I have acquired wisdom and new skills that will serve us well. I will teach my children that a bright, safe future awaits them. As I move beyond fear and humiliation, so too do my children.

My children will wear golden armor.

Nevermore will they experience the betrayals born of fear and shame. Nevermore will violence hold sway in their world. My children will learn the power that love has to shape their world. I will teach them to love themselves so that they may foil the assaults of any who seek to diminish them through aggression and contempt. They will learn that hateful words and deeds reflect the speaker's raging unmet needs and are born of starving minds. They will learn that fury and loathing have no power to contaminate their purity and goodness.

My children will wear golden armor.

My children will grow to respect their own strength and to cherish their own uniqueness. As they cherish themselves, so will they be respected and cherished by others around them.

My children will wear golden armor.

From this day on, my children are free to explore the boundless possibilities that are their entitlement. There will be difficulties and hazards along their journey, but they will be equal to them. Always will I walk beside them and they will learn to equip themselves so they may meet whatever challenges they must encounter.

My children will wear golden armor.

The love that I bear my children fills me with a new faith. I see how precious is the love that I bear them. Only now do I see how precious is the love that they bear me. The courage of my children is an inspiration to me. From this moment on, I undertake to return to my children all the love, trust, and faith that they have invested in me.

My children will wear golden armor.

Finally, I can freely give my children the greatest gifts that a mother's heart has to offer—and I shall.

My children will wear golden armor.

And so will I.

Week 36 Recorder

I have helped my children to treat themselves with love so that they may foil the assaults of any who seek to diminish them through aggression and contempt.

Monday   Date

Number of times the Step was read:
Your score:
Total score:

Tuesday   Date

Number of times the Step was read:
Your score:
Total score:

Wednesday   Date

Number of times the Step was read:
Your score:
Total score:

THURSDAY   DATE

Number of times the Step was read:

Your score:

Total score:

FRIDAY   DATE

Number of times the Step was read:

Your score:

Total score:

Your end of week score:

QUOTATION

You feel most relevant to yourself this week:

_____
_____
_____
_____
_____
_____
_____
_____

Your achievements of the week:

_____
_____
_____
_____
_____
_____
_____
_____
_____

Week 37 Recorder

I have helped my children to treat themselves with love so that they may foil the assaults of any who seek to diminish them through aggression and contempt.

Monday   DATE

Number of times the Step was read: _____

Your score: _____

Total score: _____

Tuesday   DATE

Number of times the Step was read: _____

Your score: _____

Total score: _____

Wednesday   DATE

Number of times the Step was read: _____

Your score: _____

Total score: _____

THURSDAY   DATE

Number of times the Step was read:

Your score:

Total score:

FRIDAY   DATE

Number of times the Step was read:

Your score:

Total score:

Your end of week score:

QUOTATION

You feel most relevant to yourself this week:

_____
_____
_____
_____
_____
_____
_____
_____

Your achievements of the week:

_____
_____
_____
_____
_____
_____
_____
_____

Week 38 Recorder

I have helped my children to treat themselves with love so that they may foil the assaults of any who seek to diminish them through aggression and contempt.

MONDAY   DATE

Number of times the Step was read:
Your score:
Total score:

TUESDAY   DATE

Number of times the Step was read:
Your score:
Total score:

WEDNESDAY   DATE

Number of times the Step was read:
Your score:
Total score:

THURSDAY   DATE

Number of times the Step was read:

Your score:

Total score:

FRIDAY   DATE

Number of times the Step was read:

Your score:

Total score:

Your end of week score:

QUOTATION

You feel most relevant to yourself this week:

_____
_____
_____
_____
_____
_____
_____

YOUR ACHIEVEMENTS OF THE WEEK:
_____
_____
_____
_____
_____
_____
_____
_____

Week 39 Recorder

I have helped my children to treat themselves with love so that they may foil the assaults of any who seek to diminish them through aggression and contempt.

Monday   DATE

Number of times the Step was read:
Your score:
Total score:

Tuesday   DATE

Number of times the Step was read:
Your score:
Total score:

Wednesday   DATE

Number of times the Step was read:
Your score:
Total score:

THURSDAY   DATE

Number of times the Step was read:

Your score:

Total score:

FRIDAY   DATE

Number of times the Step was read:

Your score:

Total score:

Your end of week score:

QUOTATION

You feel most relevant to yourself this week:

_____
_____
_____
_____
_____
_____
_____
_____

Your achievements of the week:

_____

_____

_____

_____

_____

_____

_____

_____

Week 40 Recorder

I have helped my children to treat themselves with love so that they may foil the assaults of any who seek to diminish them through aggression and contempt.

MONDAY   DATE

Number of times the Step was read:
Your score:
Total score:

TUESDAY   DATE

Number of times the Step was read:
Your score:
Total score:

WEDNESDAY   DATE

Number of times the Step was read:
Your score:
Total score:

THURSDAY   DATE

Number of times the Step was read:

Your score:

Total score:

FRIDAY   DATE

Number of times the Step was read:

Your score:

Total score:

Your end of week score:

QUOTATION

You feel most relevant to yourself this week:

_____

_____

_____

_____

_____

_____

_____

Your achievements of the week:

Chapter 11

Only Allow...

I'd like to honor the courage and persistence you have shown over the past months. I'd like you to honor yourself also.

You are a truly exceptional woman, you know. You've worked so hard. You've shown so much faith; you've developed such a firm foundation of self-worth. But however positively you now view yourself, rest assured that your stature is many times greater than you could ever begin to imagine.

Your potential, also, is many times greater than you could begin to imagine. Only allow yourself to believe in the unlimited abundance of your resources and you will not be disappointed. According to Herbert Otto, "We are all functioning at a small fraction of our capacity to live life fully in its total meaning of loving, caring, creating, and adventuring. Consequently, the actualizing of our potential can become the most exciting adventure of our time."

There is no reason for you to function at a small fraction of your capacity anymore. You have served your apprenticeship in suffering, in human frailty and in self-recovery, and you have learned what you need to know in order to live fully. You have learned how to love and value yourself. Until you could, there could be no hope of fully living life's total meaning of loving, caring, creating, and adventuring. Until you could, there could be no hope of your spirit soaring above the confines of past experience.

Now you are free to welcome into your life all the blessings that you desire for yourself.

Only allow the joy and beauty in your soul to resonate with the joy and beauty of the universe. And trust in all the good that lies before you. Trust in your capacity to create an adventure.

The Best is Still to Come

There was a woman who had been lovely and talented.

Three fairies had presided over her birth. The first had lavished on her a multitude of gifts and made her good and loving, beautiful and clever, sweet and endearing. But the second fairy could not bear the first, nor, given the pettiness of her vengeful nature, could she bear to think that a child should be so blessed. She used her vast powers to dash the aspirations of the first, and she bestowed upon the sleeping baby an abundance of misery. The third fairy had not the power to countermand the second and was, in truth, more than a little frightened of her, and so it was that she said the first thing that came into her mind: *"The truth shall make you free."*

The child grew up, and although she was loved by almost all who knew her, save her immediate family, she lived a life of terrible unhappiness. Her natural mother had never recovered from giving birth to her and died soon after. A wicked stepmother had stepped into the mother's shoes who treated the child exceedingly cruelly and told the father false stories to set him against his own daughter.

The child became a passionate woman who sought a love so deep and strong it would compensate for all the deprivations she had ever known. Suitors surrounded her, many of them decent, loving young men who told her of their love in measured, gentle terms. But always she was drawn to those who spoke the fairest words—for she could not know that they had the falsest, blackest hearts. One she met said that he must have her for his wife, or die in the attempt. At first he did not please her and she refused him. But he wooed her so relentlessly, and spoke such words of burning passion that she let herself be swayed. She gave herself to him with a deep and abiding love that she imagined to be a mirror of his own.

He soon tired of the prize he had won, for her chief attraction had been her unattainableness. Once he possessed her and could exert his power over her at will, she soon lost her charm for him. Increasingly he focused on her defects of character and appearance. Her eyes were too blue, her hair was too long, her breasts too full, her nature too loving, her care for their children too great. She was too womanly, too intelligent, too voluptuous, too assertive, too dependent, too stupid; she was, in short, too much a presence in his world, and his hostility to her grew daily.

His children, too, he resented increasingly; they were too loud or too quiet, too dependent, too affectionate, too time-consuming, too demanding, too childish.

He visited, first on his wife and then on his children also, all the fury that had ever smoldered in his soul, and the more he gave voice to it the greater it grew.

He passed from angry words to angry gestures and from angry gestures to evermore violent deeds. And always he ascribed blame for his violent furies to his wife. It happened, he maintained, because she had said, or not said, a certain thing; because she had looked at him, or not looked at him, in a particular way; because she had done, or failed to do, something whose significance was apparent only to him.

The wife's spirit was ever more crushed by his brutality and she became as careless of herself as he was of her. The harsher his treatment of her became, the more she came to believe in her own vileness, and the more she felt that she needed him. He, at least, was possessed of the strengths and virtues she so lamentably lacked. His presence served to hide her unworthiness from view in the world outside and she was grateful to dwell in his shadow.

She had become, she felt, no more than a ghost; the vibrant woman she once had been was dead and buried.

And so the man felt free to harm her in any way he pleased. With each assault he made on her, his indifference grew; whether she lived or died mattered but little to him. His brutalization grew daily and his fondness for his children also waned.

Still the woman clung to him in hope, against all sense. With all the strength of her passionate nature, she clung to her memory of the lover he had once been, clung to the vision of the man he might have been and might yet be. She held fast to memories until the threat he posed to her life and her children's future became so great that she could gainsay it no more.

At last she drove her husband from her. But, for a long time after, he lived on in her heart and mind. He lived on in every contemptuous thought she had for herself, in her every utterance that her life was over. He lived on in her belief that there could be no future for a creature as debased as she was, in her fear for her children's future, in her regret that their mother was such a hapless wretch.

Yet her spirit would not die. Her passion for life smoldered but it would not be extinguished. For months and even years she could do little enough to feed it or nurture herself. But during that time she tended a patch of wasteland with infinite care. Her ceaseless toil transformed it into a garden of almost magical beauty, and slowly, almost imperceptibly, the work healed her battered soul.

The day came when she welcomed the morning so that she could observe the growth her plants had made overnight. Then awareness grew in her that even she could look forward with joyful anticipation to pleasure that the morrow might bring, that she too had contributed to the beauty of the place in which she lived. So it was that she came to believe that the universe still held a promise of joys to come for her also. And that truth set her free from the prison of her past.

Step 10

The Best is Still to Come.

No more will I worry what the future will hold for me, for this I cannot know. No more will I seek to imagine how my future might look, when even my dreams and my imaginings are stunted by the perspective of the past. Such attempts serve me not, for they only project my present limitations onto an unknowable future. Such a narrow vision risks blinding me to all the, as yet, unguessed opportunities that will present themselves along my path. Instead, I will trust in a better future for I have been given the ability to create a future that will truly nurture the person that I am. As I reclaim my gifts and frailties, my future will grow ever richer.

The Best Is Still To Come.

No more will I project present worries onto an unknown future. No more will I suffer in the belief that in years and even decades to come the problems that afflict me now will afflict me still.

As I have grown from infancy to womanhood, so will I continue to grow and change. For too long I nursed the vision of an immutable world of relentless hardship and struggle. From this moment on, I repudiate that vision. So immured in misery was I, for so long, that I had forgotten that change is one of humanity's few certainties.

Henceforth I will greet change gladly for I know that those who dread change and resist its advances will be ravaged by it—while those who welcome it with open arms will be rewarded with the prizes that it brings. What these prizes are it is not for me presently to know, any more than it is possible to see the flower that has yet to develop in the tiny bud, but my faith is unassailable and I will value fully and give thanks gratefully for what I receive. And I shall hold on to the thought that whatever the future offers is but a bud that I can nurse into a beautiful bloom.

The Best Is Still To Come.

No more will I mourn the loss of my youth and beauty, for they brought me to where I am today. Had I been made differently, physically and spiritually, my circumstances would have posed challenges of a different order. I believe that everyone is set a lesson to learn and I am willing now to accept all the teachings that mine can offer me. For too long I resisted the teaching and lamented the cruelty I had experienced; now I will accept that even that cruelty served to enrich my spirit and I will be free to move on.

No more will I regret that I am no longer that young creature on the brink of life, for I have gained more wisdom, humility, and compassion than once I could even imagine. What I have lost of the freshness of my countenance is more than compensated by the blossoming of my spirit, the depth of my care for my fellows. I believe that the love and care I now feel will attract more blessings and more love into my life than ever did a pleasing appearance.

The Best Is Still to Come.

What these blessings will be I cannot know, else they would not be blessings. Nor will I seek to dictate what grace I would have bestowed on me. No longer will I fix my mind on any perceived good, for it is not given to me to know what would confer true joy and meaning on my life. In the past I have been presumptuous enough to suppose that I had the wisdom to choose my ultimate good and I have wasted precious time and energy in futile pursuit of an illusion. I know now that my wisdom lies in my openness to receive what is best in each moment and each day. Wisdom lies, above all else, not in mourning the past, but in rejoicing in the present and welcoming the future.

The Best Is Still to Come.

From this day on, I will remember that I am the architect of my own life. My mind is given daily into my charge and it is for me to make of each day what I will. My thoughts cannot be predetermined by anyone save myself. My thoughts have the power to color my days; whether they are monochrome or bright-hued is a choice that none can make but me. I choose now to paint my world with the vibrant colors of joy, serenity, gratitude, and love.

No past suffering can condemn me now to endure only a ceaseless flow of drabness and misery. None can rob me of the preciousness of each passing day. Henceforth I will celebrate daily that life still lies before me and I will explore gratefully all the promises it holds.

The Best Is Still To Come.

My life is not like a small pitcher that holds only a limited measure of joys that I must be fearful of consuming too swiftly, lest I am left thirsting for what I may never have again. Now my eyes are open to all the joys that this world affords, and their abundance amazes me. However many joys I claim for myself will neither diminish their store nor deprive my fellow creatures of their entitlement. My delight in the setting sun cannot rob another of that ephemeral splendor, but it may serve to rouse another poor creature such as I once was from their trance of misery—for joy begets only joy.

The Best is Still to Come.

From this day on, I will open up my mind and loosen my hold on things past; and my past will loosen its hold on me also. I will walk away from the gloomy dungeon in which it once sequestered me and I will step gladly towards the bright promise of the future. No more will I heed the echoes of cruel voices from the past, however much they may clamor for my attention, for they would only lure me back into that gloomy cell and rob me of the riches of the days to come. Henceforth I will safeguard my future from the many ravages of things past and I will give free rein to my potential.

The Best is Still to Come.

In the past I have forced myself to exist in the element of another. Now I choose daily the elements most congenial to me. I choose light and air, space and freedom; I will live from this moment on in a world that provides the sustenance I need. From this moment on I take charge of my present and future days, and my stewardship over my own life suffices to fill each day with wonder.

THE BEST IS STILL TO COME FOR I AM BUT THE EMBRYO OF THE WOMAN I WILL BE.

Week 41 Recorder

I opened up my mind and loosened my hold on things past, and my past also lost its hold on me. I walked away from the gloomy dungeon in which it had once sequestered me and I stepped gladly towards the bright promise of the future.

Monday   Date

Number of times the Step was read:
Your score:
Total score:

Tuesday   Date

Number of times the Step was read:
Your score:
Total score:

Wednesday   Date

Number of times the Step was read:
Your score:
Total score:

THURSDAY   DATE

Number of times the Step was read:

Your score:

Total score:

FRIDAY   DATE

Number of times the Step was read:

Your score:

Total score:

Your end of week score:

QUOTATION

You feel most relevant to yourself this week:

_____
_____
_____
_____
_____
_____
_____

Your achievements of the week:

_____
_____
_____
_____
_____
_____
_____
_____
_____

Week 42 Recorder

I opened up my mind and loosened my hold on things past, and my past also lost its hold on me. I walked away from the gloomy dungeon in which it had once sequestered me and I stepped gladly towards the bright promise of the future.

Monday   Date

Number of times the Step was read:
Your score:
Total score:

Tuesday   Date

Number of times the Step was read:
Your score:
Total score:

Wednesday   Date

Number of times the Step was read:
Your score:
Total score:

THURSDAY   DATE

Number of times the Step was read:

Your score:

Total score:

FRIDAY   DATE

Number of times the Step was read:

Your score:

Total score:

Your end of week score:

QUOTATION

You feel most relevant to yourself this week:

_____

_____

_____

_____

_____

_____

_____

Your achievements of the week:
_____
_____
_____
_____
_____
_____
_____
_____

Week 43 Recorder

I opened up my mind and loosened my hold on things past, and my past also lost its hold on me. I walked away from the gloomy dungeon in which it had once sequestered me and I stepped gladly towards the bright promise of the future.

MONDAY   DATE

Number of times the Step was read:
Your score:
Total score:

TUESDAY   DATE

Number of times the Step was read:
Your score:
Total score:

WEDNESDAY   DATE

Number of times the Step was read:
Your score:
Total score:

THURSDAY   DATE

Number of times the Step was read:

Your score:

Total score:

FRIDAY   DATE

Number of times the Step was read:

Your score:

Total score:

Your end of week score:

QUOTATION

You feel most relevant to yourself this week:

_____
_____
_____
_____
_____
_____
_____
_____

Your achievements of the week:

_____
_____
_____
_____
_____
_____
_____
_____

Week 44 Recorder

I opened up my mind and loosened my hold on things past, and my past also lost its hold on me. I walked away from the gloomy dungeon in which it had once sequestered me and I stepped gladly towards the bright promise of the future.

Monday   Date

Number of times the Step was read: _____

Your score: _____

Total score: _____

Tuesday   Date

Number of times the Step was read: _____

Your score: _____

Total score: _____

Wednesday   Date

Number of times the Step was read: _____

Your score: _____

Total score: _____

THURSDAY   DATE

Number of times the Step was read:

Your score:

Total score:

FRIDAY   DATE

Number of times the Step was read:

Your score:

Total score:

Your end of week score:

QUOTATION

You feel most relevant to yourself this week:

_____
_____
_____
_____
_____
_____
_____
_____

Your achievements of the week:
_____
_____
_____
_____
_____
_____
_____
_____

Week 45 Recorder

I opened up my mind and loosened my hold on things past, and my past also lost its hold on me. I walked away from the gloomy dungeon in which it had once sequestered me and I stepped gladly towards the bright promise of the future.

Monday   Date

Number of times the Step was read:
Your score:
Total score:

Tuesday   Date

Number of times the Step was read:
Your score:
Total score:

Wednesday   Date

Number of times the Step was read:
Your score:
Total score:

THURSDAY   DATE

Number of times the Step was read:

Your score:

Total score:

FRIDAY   DATE

Number of times the Step was read:

Your score:

Total score:

Your end of week score:

QUOTATION

You feel most relevant to yourself this week:

_____
_____
_____
_____
_____
_____
_____
_____

Your achievements of the week:

_____
_____
_____
_____
_____
_____
_____
_____

Chapter 12

I Am a Miracle

The time has come to rejoice at the person you have grown into, the unique, extraordinary human being you are. It's got nothing to do with old-fashioned notions you were probably brought up with about not having too high an opinion of yourself. It's about loving yourself and acknowledging your true worth. Rejoice every day in your gifts and your blessings and they will only multiply.

What follows is by no means an exhaustive list, but you can add to it as appropriate, because you are a miracle.

Because I have come through the death of the spirit...
    And yet have chosen life;
Because I have known much despair...
    Yet I have chosen hope;
Because I was once a victim...
    And am now a survivor;
Because I was imprisoned...
    And yet have claimed my freedom;
Because I was made dumb...
    Yet now speak with a voice that none may silence;
Because I once hid my face in the shadows...
    Yet now rejoice in the light;
Because I could not defend myself from cruelty...
    Yet I clothe my children in golden armor;
Because I have endured the starvation of the heart...
    Yet share my love gladly with my fellows;
Because contempt came near to suffocating my soul...
    Yet I cherish my uniqueness;
Because I was taught to be worthless...
    And have learned I am irreplaceable;
I am a miracle.

What a long way you've come. Are you at your journey's end? Not unless you choose to stop here - for the road stretches out ahead of you as far as the eye can see. Your journey has become a magnificent voyage of self-recovery. You have reclaimed so much of your potential, and the more of your potential you use, the more you have. So why would you want to stop here when you have so much to offer to yourself and to those around you?

You no longer need me to walk beside you, although my support, my faith, and my boundless admiration for all that you have achieved remain with you. But now it is for you to share the gift of who you have become along the way with those who will benefit from it—and appreciate the wonder of you and themselves.

I thank you for the privilege you have shared with me of accompanying you along your way. I leave you with the words of Eileen Caddy: "Expect your every need to be met, expect abundance on every level, expect to grow spiritually."

Next Steps

It has been a pleasure working with you through *"The Woman You Want To Be"*.

Now that you have completed the course, where do you go from here?

If you want to spend more time understanding the nature of abusers as well as the inner workings of abusive relationships, you will find books and programs on my website **www.recoverfromemotionalabuse.com** to help you.

My book, *"Married to Mr Nasty"* lays bare the reality of abusive relationships. Plus, you will find courses on *"Relationship Red Flags"*, and *"How to Create More Happiness, Starting Now"* as well as my flagship, *"Escape From The Abusive Kingdom"* course on the dynamics of abusive relationships.

If you feel that the time has come to explore in more depth your own issues – either about a past toxic relationship or how you create a healthy, loving relationship in the future, then email me at:
annie@recoverfromemotionalabuse.com.

You have a come a long way. But, please, don't mistake where you are now for the journey's end.

You had to grow *out* of the misery of the past. Now you can continue to grow through joy.

Don't settle for second best. Don't settle for just *existing*. You have a right to enjoy your own life.

Warm wishes for your happiness,

Annie

Printed in Great Britain
by Amazon